7/1/99 – Bernie Stinson,

The book is easy to read and interesting.

Hope you'll enjoy it!

Ronnie Corn

Copyright © 1996 by John Kretschmer

ISBN 0-9655684-0-7

Library of Congress Catalog Card Number 96-090921

Published by Fortuna Publications
P.O. Box 519
Ft. Lauderdale, FL 33302

Library of Congress Cataloging-in-Publication Data

Kretschmer, John
A DIFFERENT DRUMMER / by John Kretschmer - 1st edition
Biography Industrial Drums
Shipping Containers

Manufactured in The United States of America

FIRST EDITION

It took courage to stand up to the American steel industry, especially during the 1950's and 60's when the steel industry was one of the most powerful organizations in the country. It took foresight to purchase steel from a fledgling industrial nation like Japan in 1960 and risk your entire manufacturing operation on an untested, 12,000 mile delivery schedule. It took fortitude to beat back challenges from aggressive trade unions while maintaining incredible employee loyalty. And, it took imagination to consistently stay ahead of your competitors with innovation and engineering excellence. These are the ingredients at play in A DIFFERENT DRUMMER.

Robert Evans is a larger than life figure who took over a failing backyard cooperage business during the heart of the depression and built it into one of the largest industrial drum manufacturing, reconditioning and filling operations in the world. The story is set in New Orleans and the unique flavor and rhythm of the city is pervasive. Also included are a series of caustic episodes written by Robert Evans nearly twenty year ago that describe some of the less that forthright inner workings of the steel industry in the past. A DIFFERENT DRUMMER chronicles one man's extraordinary life and reminds us that the American dream is still achievable.

TABLE OF CONTENTS

THE ROBERT EVANS STORY

A

DIFFERENT

DRUMMER

By John Kretschmer

BY ARTHUR J. SCHULTZ

My first meeting with Bob Evans took place almost twenty years ago. A few months earlier I had been elected President of the Steel Shipping Container Institute (SSCI). This trade association represents steel drum manufacturers. At the time of our meeting Bob Evans was in the new drum business as well as a reconditioner of used drums.

Soon after I started with SSCI I made the recruiting of new members one of my top priorities. Membership in the Institute had dropped dangerously low - only twenty-members. My strategy was to attend meetings where I might meet prospective members for the Institute. In the fall of 1977 I attended the meeting of the Petroleum Packaging Committee and this was my first opportunity to meet Bob Evans. He was very cordial and we had a good discussion on various issues facing both new drum manufacturers and reconditioners.

Bob Evans had never been a member of SSCI. I reviewed the advantages of membership and the ambitious plans I had for the future. His main concern with SSCI as well as NABADA (National Barrel and Drum Association, a trade group for reconditioners) was their inability to work together. Unfortunately, the Presidents of these two associations were not even on speaking terms. I told Bob Evans that I had called Morris Herschon, the head of NABADA, and had invited him to a working luncheon. Morris Herschon and I talked of developing plans to work together, particularly on issues where we had joint interests. At this time I suggested to Morris that he invite me to speak at the next meeting of NABADA Board of Directors and conversely, I would invite him to speak to our members at our next quarterly meeting scheduled for January 1978 in New Orleans.

Bob Evans agreed that the plans as outlined above were good ones but he was doubtful that these plans could be accomplished. He further said that if I was successful in speaking to the NABADA Board he would join SSCI. At the next NABADA meeting I did indeed make a presentation which was well received and we agreed to work together for our mutual interests. The next day I wrote a letter to Bob Evans and explained what had happened at the NABADA meeting. The very same day he mailed in his application and became a member of SSCI. Bob Evans is a man of his word and this is only one example, there are many more.

In January 1978, he attended his first SSCI meeting in New Orleans, just across the river from his plant. From that point on he took a strong interest in all SSCI programs and never missed an official meeting. He never hesitated to offer strong advice on the many issues that faced the Institute. He supplied members of his staff to serve on various committees and supported the Institute programs. He was dedicated to improving the quality of steel drums.

FOREWORD

In my long association with Bob Evans I found him to be a strong family man. He is a self-made man, very innovative, fair with his employees and a very good business man. All of these worthwhile traits originated from a man who started with very little and through hard work, strong leadership, good business acumen and sound ethics, became a leader in both the new steel drum and reconditioning industries.

A.J.S.

October 1996

CHAPTER ONE

AN ELUSIVE QUEST

The blue and white structures of Evans Industries in Harvey, Louisiana resist easy classification as they sprawl across both sides of Peters Road, a narrow, bustling industrial artery. Evans is a microcosm of the big city across the river, New Orleans, the city from which the company draws its strength and its soul. And like the legendary river that springs from a small stream and gradually meanders and widens into a mighty delta, Evans too has charted its own, unique course. From humble beginnings to industrial heavyweight, Evans has expanded steadily. Evans has grown the old fashioned way, not from hostile acquisitions or leveraged buy outs but from within, from sweat, innovation, engineering excellence and from tirelessly pouring profits back into the company in a relentless pursuit of market share.

The Evans infrastructure in Harvey, a rambling collection of factories, warehouses, cranes, trucks, barges and office buildings, dominates the landscape from the vantage point of a Lapalco Boulevard over pass. From this perspective it is difficult to imagine Evans' inauspicious beginnings. The company staggered to life almost sixty years ago during the heart of the Great Depression as a small backyard cooperage. In those days the Evans family collected wooden lard barrels by horse and wagon and repaired and cleaned them by hand over an open fire in nearby Gretna. Today, Evans Industries Inc., is one of America's largest manufacturers, reconditioners, fillers and distributors of steel drums and in addition to the Harvey facility, has plants in Houston, Texas, and Cushing, Oklahoma and supplies knockdown drums for international assembly plants.

Fifty-five gallon steel drums may not seem romantic but they are the container of choice, the unsung workhorse for Industry throughout the world. Invented by the irrepressible Nellie Bly nearly a century ago, the steel drum industry shows no signs of slowing down, there is no other container product on the horizon ready to render drums obsolete. From drums of cooking oil destined for remote African villages to lubricants bound for high tech Asian automotive plants, to toxic chemicals that must be transported in safe reliable containers, international commerce beats to the tune of a 55 gallon steel drum. And while Evans now makes more money building new drums, which they fill and facilitate distribution on a global scale, the reconditioning plant which lies astride the Harvey Canal, a vital man made conduit to the Mississippi River, is in many ways still the soul of the company.

In a world increasingly dominated by software, there is nothing soft about reconditioning steel drums and many manufacturers have abandoned reconditioning altogether. Reconditioning is a loud and gritty job, a hard job, but this is what industrial recycling is all about. The slogan posted neatly on the outside of the plant says it all, "Reconditioning: Resource Conservation." Evans is one of the largest reconditioners in the world. Used drums are collected from all over the south by Evans' distinctive trucks, which are about the longest trucks on the road today and are delivered to the Evans plant in Harvey or to a newer plant in Houston. Drums that other reconditioners won't touch Evans renews. Drums that might have been filled with chemicals that nobody else wants to talk about much less recondition are not cut up for scrap, or worse, sealed away in a mysterious landfill, they are made serviceable again. If you claim to be a reconditioner, you should be able to recondition just about anything and do it in a manner so that both the company and the environment end up with a net profit.

Reconditioning drums is much tougher than it used to be when the industry really emerged in the 1940's and 50's. Petroleums and vegetable oils, drum contents of old, were relatively easy to clean and the environmental ethos that permeates every aspect of industry today had not yet swept the country. The chemicals that are shipped in drums today are a different story and consequently reconditioning drums has never been more important from an environmental standpoint.

Used drums follow a tortuous path before they are declared reconditioned. They begin by being either scoured by high pressure rotary water washers or baked in a computer monitored scorching inferno called a drum reclamation furnace. Then the drums are hydraulically dedented and the interiors and exteriors are shot blasted and chained clean. The drums are submersion tested for leaks and after a fresh coat of paint, neatly stacked and ready for service once again.

Everything that can possibly be salvaged during the reconditioning process is reused, right down to the paint scrapings, which are collected, recycled and ultimately reapplied in the finishing stage. Lets face it, Evans reconditions steel drums to make money but this is the kind of resource renewal that makes dollars and sense in today's world. It is also part of the commitment Evans has made to be involved in every aspect of the steel drum business and gives a hint of where the company is going in the future. Evans won't abandon reconditioning, it will develop technology to make the process cleaner and more profitable. That has been their track record for six decades.

The Harvey new drum plant is across the street. The high speed line can, in a pinch, produce 800 drums per hour but is more comfortable running about 550. It is consistently one of the fastest drum lines in the world. Just ask Bobby Trilla, the confident young plant manager whose lineage in the drum business goes back more than half a century. "Nobody can match our overall production month to month," Trilla declares, "and," he insists, "we can even go faster." Blue gray coils of premium steel begin at one end of the uniquely designed three story plant. They are unrolled, cut, formed and seam welded. Gradually both light and heavy gauge raw steel starts to resemble drums which march like little toy soldiers from station to station. Innovation is evident throughout this plant. From the line that nests knockdown drums waiting to be exported in mass, to an in-house designed and built state-of-the-art helium leak detector, to a breakthrough designed, Monolithic Closure System that will replace standard flanges, Evans has clawed its way to the top in the fiercely competitive new drum business.

The fill plant is just down the road from the new drum plant. Evans was the first and is still the only drum company to combine reconditioning, new drum manufacturing, filling, warehousing and distribution in one efficient operation. Of course it helps to be the only major drum company in the south located on the water. Evans fills over 400,000 drums a year with diverse products, including hazardous and highly flammable materials, affectionately nicknamed, "diethyl double death." There is simply no margin for error when dealing with these dangerous chemicals. The carefully metered filling process is highly sophisticated and the drums must never leak. Evans does this job right and accepts the huge responsibility that it must continue to do the job right. They can also store another 30,000 drums in on site warehouses, and this is just the Harvey operation, the numbers go up when you add the production of Evans' Houston and Cushing plants to the mix.

During, and especially right after WW II, three major steel companies were players in the drum business in New Orleans. It is not an exaggeration to say that the 'Big Easy' was both the jazz and fifty-five gallon drum capitol of the world. Huge amounts of petroleum products were shipped from the port which was fast becoming America's busiest. The oil was originally needed to keep the Allied Armed Forces on the move and then later, to keep up with the insatiable demands of the Marshall Plan and the rebuilding of Asia. Evans was just a small reconditioner and hauler at this time and the reconditioning business was bottoming out. Drums that were shipped overseas did not return to New Orleans for reconditioning.

Evans, a scrawny new kid on a block dominated by big bullies, resolved to enter the saturated new drum market. Initially the intent was just to build drums for their fledgling filling operation. However, Evans quickly became a major drum manufacturer, and the company president and founder was forced to take on the drum divisions of the powerful American Steel Industry head on. How Evans Cooperage challenged and beat the giants of the steel industry is just part of this story, part of the legend of Robert Evans and the fiercely independent company that bears his name. He was a giant slayer, a David among Goliaths and like David, Robert Evans never backed down from a fight when the cause was just. And like David again, his success story is unlikely and compelling. This book chronicles the life of Robert (Bob) Evans and in the process documents a classic American tale of triumph, (albeit spiced with the unique flavor of New Orleans) the little guy beating the big guys, but it is also much more than that. Robert Evans' story also demonstrates that it is possible to succeed in business by employing unquestioned integrity and unflinching honesty, subjects not at the top of the course syllabus in Entrepreneurship 101 at Harvard Business School but principles upon which Bob Evans built his business and lived his life.

The corporate offices are also on this, the east side of Peters Road, across a narrow parking lot from the plant. There is no glass tower here, in fact, driving down Peters Road it is easy to mistake the world headquarters of Evans Industries Inc., for another small plant or warehouse. Evans is not a company where paper pushers thrive, this is a company where the managers of the Reconditioning and New Drum Manufacturing Divisions have their offices in the plants. To say the executive offices are spartan is an overstatement. But the man who built this company was not the kind of manager who avoided the din of the plant, indeed, for many years Bob Evans personally knew the operator of every piece of machinery that he owned and was never shy or particularly quiet about offering advice if he felt productivity could be improved. Bob Evans micro managed his company before there was even a term for such things and he never thought of Peters Road or the parking lot as a boundary, it was not a barrier between classes. The men and women in suits had better understand what the men and women with hard hats were doing. Bob Evans was not afraid to cross Peters Road, his own beginnings were too humble and his successes too hard won to worry about appearances or to ever feel secure in the volatile drum business.

Horace Williams, the manager of the Reconditioning Division, a big, strapping African American with a throaty laugh tells a story about Bob Evans crossing Peters Road. "I'd been hired as a Production Supervisor and had been with the company just a year or two. Now this is going back, fifteen maybe twenty years ago, so Mr. Evans was in his mid-sixties then. There was a guy in the plant who just wasn't pulling his weight and I had to let him go.

He didn't take it well. I told him to leave the plant immediately. Well, he came after me with a steel pipe but I saw him coming and I was able to defend myself and escort him out of the plant. That night, when I was getting ready to go home, the guy confronts me at the door, with his two brothers. Things were going to be ugly. I'm big, but so were these guys and there were three of them."

"Well there were only a few people in the plant, and when they saw the scene developing they disappeared. I figured I was in for a beating. But somebody, thank God, must have called over to the offices, because the next thing I knew, Bob Evans himself was sprinting across Peters Road, holding a 38 caliber pistol over his head and hollering like wild man, "hold on Horace, just hold on." Well these guys took one look at Mr. Evans, his white hair standing straight up, his face flush with rage and his finger on that trigger and they took off for good. To say Mr. Evans looks after his employees is putting it mildly."

Jimmy Richoux, originally from Larose, Louisiana, a sleepy Cajun town on the banks of Bayou Lafourche, has been with the company for over 30 years. Today he is Vice President of Purchasing. Richoux remembers another time Bob Evans crossed Peters Road. An employee had fallen off a company barge into the Harvey Canal and was flailing about in the water - he couldn't swim. While his co-workers frantically threw him lines, an emergency call was made to the office. "There is a man drowning," was all Bob Evans needed to hear. "We all ran over there," Jimmy explains, "but Bob was way out in front of us. As he ran he ripped off his jacket and shirt and kicked off his shoes. Without breaking stride he dove into the Canal," Jimmy paused here, "you've seen the Harvey Canal? Well this was twenty, twenty-five years ago when it was really polluted. Anyway, the man has gone down. Bob, who was no spring chicken, he must have been close to sixty at the time, dove down over and over again but he couldn't find the poor guy, couldn't save him. The fire department arrived and insisted that Bob get out of the water and finally fished him out with a big net. Shaking like a wet dog, he was furious, he couldn't believe he hadn't saved the man's life and he couldn't believe the man had been so stupid as to fall into the canal in the first place. That's quintessential Bob Evans."

This is the story of a man and a company and two are not easily separated. Love him or loathe him, Bob Evans staked out his territory in the drum business, which has never been an easy business, and took on all comers. No one ever doubted where Bob Evans stood on an issue and his were usually the only comments at either the Association of Container Reconditioners or Steel Shipping Container Institute functions that everybody listened to because they were sure to raise a commotion and spark heated responses. Ironically his message was invariably one of conciliation, that new drum manufacturers and reconditioners should work together instead of being perpetual adversaries, but this is like asking the Arabs and Israelis, or the English and the Irish to stop fighting. As logical as it may seem, it is not likely to happen and this lack of cooperation frustrated Bob Evans and he was never shy about letting people know it.

"The man simply makes decisions," explains Ty Techera, now a consultant for Evans and a long time friend and associate. "I remember calling on Evans when I was just out of college. I was selling drum flanges and other fittings imported from Taiwan. I gave my pitch but was politely turned down and the purchasing agent sent me on my way. As I was leaving the office, I literally bumped into Bob Evans. He asked what I was doing there and I told him I was selling flanges. 'Well who have you sold them to already?' he asked in his abrupt way. When I mentioned that his competitor in Houston had just bought a container load he stopped and looked me squarely in the eyes. 'Then I'll take three,' he said without hesitation. I said "three, three what?" 'Three containers,' he said irritated that I was wasting his time, and just like that he was gone. A few months later there was a strike and domestic steel and flange prices went through the roof but Bob Evans had a complete inventory on hand."

While his competitors have no doubt cursed him from time to time, especially when one of his innovations caught them off guard, his employees, and today there are nearly 500, have been remarkably loyal. This is in many ways, their story too. That may sound like a cliche but it isn't, just ask Pablo Maique. Maique escaped from Cuba in 1966, on one of the last freedom flights and today he runs the machine shop. Maique, who began as washer in the reconditioning plant credits Bob Evans with having the foresight and kindness to overlook the simple fact that he couldn't speak English when he first applied for a job. "Mr. Evans could tell I knew my way around a machine shop and he took a chance on me. I was most grateful. He also encouraged me to work on my English," Maique says today in good, but heavily accented English, "but in the meantime he knew I had a family to support and was willing to judge me on my ability. I put in eighty hour weeks in those days and before long I was on my feet."

Two years ago, the Amalgamated Clothing and Textile Workers of the AFL/CIO attempted to organize Evans. The labor bosses thought they had a sure thing. The company was just too large not to be unionized, the management was not politically connected and there had been an ugly strike and much labor unrest back in the early sixties. And besides, most of the plant workers are African Americans and Evans, a privately held concern, is owned by a white family.

The company looked ripe. There seemed room for discontentment but the stereotypes just didn't fit. They often don't in the south, especially in someplace as unpredictable as New Orleans. The Union just didn't get it, most of the employees were quite satisfied at Evans. Without question Evans workers put in long hours, sometimes excruciatingly so. But after forty hours they are working on time and a half and at the end of the week they take home hefty paychecks. Many of the hourly workers in the plant make more money than some of the managers across the street. If you want to make money at Evans, you can, but you have to earn it, you have to sweat for it. In the end the Union gave up and left town seven days before the scheduled election. They knew they were in for a beating, they simply did not have the support of the employees and figured it was better to sneak away than to lose by ballot.

I have been told that the American Dream, a hackneyed phrase these days, is changing and so are the entrepreneurs who chase it. The vision is more elusive. Maybe that is true. Bob Evans considers himself a practical man, a man of action, a business man, certainly not a dreamer. But like it or not, he navigated a classic, though rarely traveled highway, he made his way down that often talked about road that leads to Shangri-la, a quintessential American rags to riches story.

Against incredible odds he used street smarts, relentless hard work, a formidable imagination, an aversion to the status quo and, most importantly, unquestioned integrity to build a major manufacturing company. He took some losses and suffered some failures along the way, but he always kept forging ahead. He was never afraid to take calculated risks and never afraid to bear the consequences. His greatest accomplishment may be that while many industrial firms of his era have plunged into despair, disrepair or even bankruptcy, Evans Industries is still prospering and strategically positioned in every aspect of the drum business.

The torch has been passed to his son Ronnie, and that flame should burn well into the new millennium. "My father's greatest strength," says Ronnie, who like his father grew up in the drum business, "is that he never lost his vision, he always steered a well charted course. With that said though, he was also very decisive, in fact at times impulsive, but his rare ability to keep the big picture in focus while acting swiftly in dealing with the day to day demands of running the business was the key to the company's success."

I am not sure that Ronnie or today's entrepreneurs in general, have the same range of options that Bob Evans had during the formative years of Evans Cooperage. Industrial companies today and the managers who run them must constantly balance the pursuit of profits with rapidly changing social and environmental responsibilities. I suspect however, that the basic ingredients that comprise the American Dream really have not changed very much, it just takes a special person to stir them up. This is a story about one of those special people.

CHAPTER TWO

A BACKYARD COOPERAGE

Responsibility has a penurious way of cutting childhood short, of nudging children head first into the sometimes harsh and always uncertain world of adulthood. On a cool autumn evening in 1930, Bob Evans had responsibility thrust upon him like a cold dagger and his childhood came to an abrupt end. He was eighteen years old.

Just before dark he climbed aboard the Algiers ferry at the foot of Canal Street, not far from the Poydras Street Wharf, just as he had done all fall. After crossing to the West Bank, he made his way home to the small frame house in Gretna in a neighborhood of shotgun houses not far from the levy that held back the river. He was attending Spencer Business School downtown. He was an indifferent student, not particularly adept at typing, shorthand, bookkeeping, and the other essential skills that were supposed to transform him from capricious youth to earnest business clerk.

The only reason he was in school at all was to please his mother, who had desperately wanted her first born son to pursue a university education. A proud woman, Beulah Witzman Evans viewed education as the only vehicle that could change her children's unpromising prospects in those early depression years. She wanted Bob to escape the physical labors of a factory job by working in an office. Although the pay was about equal, in the 1930's an entry level office job was considered a giant leap up the social ladder.

However, after finishing high school near the bottom of his class and with the family's small cooperage business constantly teetering on the edge of bankruptcy, university was not an option, business school was a barely affordable alternative. Bob, who loved to read and did so incessantly although not what he was assigned to read, just wasn't cut out for the dull regimen of higher education. With the end of the semester near, he was seriously considering the prospect of quitting school. "I'll never be a businessman," he told himself, but the thought of disappointing his mother troubled him deeply as he waffled over enrolling for the next semester.

When he pushed open the screen door and stepped into the house that night any notions of his continuing school were dashed. He found his mother hunched in a rocking chair, sobbing bitterly. He rushed to her side and cradled her in his arms. She was holding a note, a suicide note. Earlier that day Bob's father had tried to take his own life by drinking caustic soda. The attempt failed, he was found in time and rushed to the hospital but the effect on the Evans family, in particular Bob and his mother was profound. His father was lucky to be alive but he was a broken man, he had suffered a complete nervous breakdown and needed professional help. Suddenly, Bob not only had a distraught mother and seriously ill father to look after but also three younger brothers and a sister to support as well. As if by decree the family responsibility had been tossed into his lap.

A BACKYARD COOPERAGE

Robert Evans was born on November 27, 1912 delivered at home by a midwife. He came into the world, screaming no doubt, in a small house partially built with Mississippi River barge board and decorated with a simple lattice work over the stoop on 11th Street in Gretna, Louisiana. Gretna was and still is a working class town. In those days, Gretna was more of a river town and the river brought not only occasional flood waters but also a steady flow of immigrants. The Evans lived in a German section of Gretna. Ironically, some of those stout hearted Germans (along with other mostly Irish immigrants) had come to New Orleans as laborers to dig the Harvey Canal, the same canal that would one day float barges carrying thousands of Evans drums to waiting ships for distribution throughout the world.

The earliest picture of Bob Evans shows him at age two standing protectively next to his brother Charles, later to be known as Buddy. Bob has flowing shoulder length hair and penetrating eyes. Bob Evans' earliest memories are of swimming in the river, eating his mother's homemade pies, going to school and occasionally, church. Like most people in Louisiana in the early 1900's, Bob Evans was ostensibly a Catholic. However, after his baptism he did not spend a lot of time in church. Instead he played with his brothers and sisters and as he got older and a little more daring he roamed the neighborhood with his pals, Albert and Eddie Drinkhouse. They hunted rabbits in what was then swampy forest land but is today the nearby country club community where he lives. This was a time before we parceled people into specific social and economic divisions. The Evans were part of a huge, hard working lower middle class. They never had a lot of money but the children went to school in clean clothes and came home to a nice supper every evening. If they were poor they didn't know it. And like most boys, Bob and his brothers worked whenever they had to and work for Bob meant the backyard cooperage business.

By all accounts Robert T. Evans, Bob's father, was an honest man, even a pious man and most certainly a nice guy. Unfortunately he was also a drunk. He battled alcoholism his entire life and never completely tamed the demon. It was alcohol that steered him toward attempted suicide and it was alcohol that would eventually cut short his life before the age of fifty. Robert T. Evans was a cooper, a barrel maker and repairer by trade. But instead of taking a steady job in one of the large barrel plants in New Orleans, he stubbornly insisted on running his own small business. His oldest son obviously inherited this same fierce sense of independence but some people are born businessmen and some are not. Unfortunately, like most people, Bob's father was one of the latter.

Robert T. Evans had converted the small stables behind the family home into a backyard cooperage. His business was relatively simple. He would purchase and repair by hand, secondhand wooden barrels that he collected by horse and wagon. Then he would sell the barrels to companies that needed shipping containers for lards, syrups, oils and occasionally during those prohibition days, whiskey. He was in fact, a reconditioner, one of the same basic enterprises that Evans continues to operate today. His operation however, was not quite on the same scale. A big black pot was the predecessor to the four stage rotary washer. Oak and gum wood barrels were literally dipped into the pot which was heated over a roaring open fire and scrubbed clean. When Mr. Evans, or one of his drivers arrived with an especially big load of barrels the entire family pitched in and scrubbed until their finger tips were raw.

Unfortunately, whenever the business would begin to prosper Robert T. Evans would drink up the profits. Prohibition or not, alcohol was relatively easy to come by in New Orleans in 1930. But during rare dry periods, Bob's father would quench his thirst for booze and steady his shaking hands with a low grade bootleg brew called, "barrel wash." Oak whiskey barrels always absorbed a small amount of the alcohol they stored and Bob's father knew all the tricks of extraction. He would pour boiling water into old barrels and then set them out in the yard and let the Louisiana sun and heat do the work. Once the 'char' settled, he would tap the barrel and have a new supply of booze, albeit some pretty rough stuff.

For Bob, his father's alcoholism was a constant embarrassment. Gretna was a small town and like most small towns there were few secrets. Bob remembers his father as one of two 'town drunks.' His school mates would whisper about his father behind his back. More than once the old man made a public fool of himself in a drunken stupor while Bob who loved his dad would silently seethe. Even his father's horse would lose patience with the old man when he was drunk. After stopping off at a neighborhood speakeasy, the elder Evans would loose track of time and shamelessly drink the night away. The poor horse would eventually give up and trot home. He would then stand stolidly in the front yard and wait for Bob or one of his brothers to come out and remove the hitch and lead him back to the stables.

On that fateful night in 1930, Bob and his mother had a long talk. She told her son that they were, for all practical purposes, broke. His father's older brother, a successful manager had agreed to pay to put Bob's father in an institution, to dry him out, but Bob would have to put bread on the family table. The Great Depression was sweeping the country and New Orleans was particularly hard hit. Bob knew that the backyard cooperage business was doomed to failure. He was lucky to find a job as a day laborer with the Chickasaw Cooperage Company. It was familiar, if unpleasant, work. He manned the line barreling lubricating oil for export. He made 30 cents an hour.

Bob's work ethic and propensity for personal sacrifice were traits he inherited from his Grandmother. Widowed at an early age, Bob's grandmother raised her two daughters on her own. They lived in a small rented house on the West Bank and Mrs. Witzman would send one of her daughters with the rent money across town to the landlord each month. One month Bob's aunt accidentally misplaced the envelope with the rent money, Mrs. Witzman always paid her bills in cash and the money was nowhere to be found. The landlord was understanding but Bob's grandmother refused to accept his sympathy much less his charity and told him simply that she would settle up with him next month. For a full month Bob's grandmother, who worked in the city, walked to work saving bus and ferry fares. She confined herself to toast and coffee, although her daughters never knew it and put the food money toward the rent. At the end of the month she proudly paid the landlord two months rent.

Bob worked ten hours a day, six days a week and brought home $15 for his labors. He kept $2 for himself and turned the rest over to his mother to support the family. It was a grueling routine but Bob accepted it stoically. He kept his precious stash stored away in a small wooden box under the rug in the bedroom he shared with his three brothers. From this meager sum, he financed his modest personal life which consisted of going to the movies once a week, regular haircuts and occasionally buying a new shirt or tie for a special occasion.

It was a shock when he came home one evening and found that one of his brothers had dipped into his box and stolen some of his money. He had a good head for figures and kept a precise mental reckoning of his savings. He was furious and confronted the offending brother. But it was too late, the damage was done, the money was spent. This seemingly trivial event was a prelude to a problematic, love/hate relationship he would have with his siblings in the years to come.

By his own admission Bob Evans was twenty years old before he ever had a drink of alcohol or kissed a girl. "I took my first drink to get up the nerve to kiss a girl." Although he still worked as a laborer most of the day, he also spent time running a small laboratory in the plant. He conducted physical tests on the lubricating oil that they drummed and more importantly, his wages were increased to forty cents an hour which allowed him to occasionally make his way into the city for a night out. Bob did his best to keep his spirits up but his modest resources did not permit any excesses. These were survival days for Bob and his family and just keeping food on the family table was an accomplishment. The swing era, as if on cue to brighten the national mood in the midst of the depression, came to life in the middle of the decade and Bob like the rest of the country was seduced by the smooth sounds. Bob occasionally joined other youngsters downtown and danced to the enthralling Big Band music at the Terrace Club. Popular New Orleans bandleaders of the time were Tony Almerico, Russ Papalia, Roy Liberto, Johnny Detroit and Sharkey Bonano.

But these joyful interludes were few and far between as Bob continued to work long and arduous hours to help support his family. For seven years he worked for the Chickasaw Cooperage Company, rarely missing a day and never arriving late. Although he didn't realize it at the time, we never do, he was learning the drum business in the best way, from the bottom up. Chickasaw was trying, unsuccessfully as it turned out, to convert from wooden barrels to steel drums which were rapidly coming to dominate the industry.

During this period Bob's father returned home and briefly went to work at a local cooperage. Swearing he would never drink again, he conned Bob's mother out of a couple hundred dollars she had miraculously managed to save and reopened the backyard business. Bob's three younger brothers went to work for their father. He paid them two dollars a week and supplied room and board. Before long Bob's father sought solace in the bottle and predictably the business began to nose dive once again. Over the years Bob had repeatedly rejected his father's desperate pleas for him to join the family business. So many times he had promised to give up drinking and so many times he failed, Bob just did not trust him and he knew that a joint venture with his father was doomed to failure. Still, in 1938 he caved in to the old man's insistent urgings. It was not that he had any false hopes that his father was ready to abandon the bottled nightmare that was ruining his life, it was that he realized that if the backyard business collapsed once more he would have to support the entire family again anyway. He had also come to the conclusion that he simply wasn't going anywhere working as a laborer, if he was ever going to change his station in life the backyard cooperage business offered a slight glimmer of opportunity. Cautiously Bob agreed to work with his father but he had two very specific conditions. First, his father had to quit drinking and secondly, Bob would call the shots and be completely in charge of the business. His father, who would not live much longer, grudgingly accepted his son's terms although he found the first condition harder to keep than the second.

Bob Evans is not an easy man to say no to and one of his first decisions upon taking over the business was to demand that everybody in the family had to work harder. Except for Leoni, his younger sister who worked in a department store selling stockings, the entire family pitched in to help the business, although his younger brothers often needed some cajoling. Small trucks had replaced horse and wagons and wooden drums were virtually obsolete but the work was still very demanding.

There were times when all four boys were out collecting drums and Bob's mother and sister were in the backyard scrubbing them clean. Unfortunately, Bob's father soon resorted to his old familiar ways and could not be relied upon to help with the business, although his antics always kept things interesting.

Despite his persistent drinking problems, Bob decided to take his father with him on an ill fated business trip to Shreveport where he had been told he could purchase a huge load of used drums at a good price. The old man, who was also very persuasive, convinced Bob that it was silly to drive their small truck all the way to Shreveport empty and insisted that they take something to sell when they arrived. He suggested they load up with oranges because a killer frost had made them hard to find in northern Louisiana, and he assured his son that they would make a handsome profit. Bob should have known better.

With the truck crammed full of oranges that had been grown south of New Orleans it took them all day in the those pre-expressway days to drive to Shreveport. They found a small tourist cabin on the outskirts of town and went to bed right after dinner, exhausted after a long day on dusty, two lane roads. Bob woke early, anxious to start pedaling oranges and buying drums but his father was not in the room. Exasperated, Bob hastily dressed and went to look for the old man. Just as Bob opened the door he heard a car squeal as the driver slammed on the brakes. He saw his father swaying across the street in a drunken haze. The car swerved and screeched to a stop but couldn't avoid glancing the old man. Bob's father was literally pitched high into the air and then ignominiously plopped down on the hood. Bob dashed out to rescue his father. They say God watches over drunks for just as Bob reached his father the old man looked at his son who was is in a state of near panic, rather indifferently, as if to say, "now Bob, don't look at me that way, it is perfectly normal to be sprawled out on the hood of a car at six in the morning."

Bob carried him on his back into the orange laden truck and rushed to the hospital. Once he realized the old man was not seriously hurt Bob was furious. He screamed and hollered at him as the doctor tended to his bumps and bruises. The doctor scolded Bob, "this man is delirious," he told him. "He's not delirious," Bob said disgustedly, "he's drunk, he's always drunk."

The doctor ordered Bob to keep his father in bed for a day or two and to apply hot compresses to his leg which was badly bruised, "the hotter the better." Back at the tourist cabin Bob put a lamp directly over his father's sore leg, to keep the compresses really hot, before departing to peddle oranges. Unfortunately, most of the grocers in town had already anticipated the orange shortage and were well stocked. Bob could hardly give them away and by the end of the day was lucky to earn back about half of what he had paid for the oranges in the first place. He was not in a good mood when he returned to the room that evening since he had wasted a whole day trying to sell oranges when what he had come to do was to buy drums. His mood blackened further when he noticed smoke billowing from the cabin window. His father was on fire! It seems the compresses were a little too hot and the old man, who was drunk again, didn't even know it. Bob extinguished the fire and wondered again, what had possessed him to bring the old man on the trip?

Fortunately, they did manage to find some used drums, a huge load of drums near the the freight yard, too many in fact for their small truck. Bob made arrangements to ship the drums back to Gretna in a railroad car. Just as he and his father, who was feeling a little better, were delivering the first load of drums to the freight yard, the truck broke down. A shortage of money either spawns despair or resourcefulness and Bob Evans is nothing if not resourceful. Sitting in his broken down truck brimming with drums Bob heard the train whistle whining in the distance and slammed the wheel in frustration. The next train south was not scheduled for days.

Regaining his composure, he jumped out of the truck and flagged down a passing truck. Unleashing all the charm he could muster, he persuaded the driver to tow his lame truck all the way back to Gretna where it could be repaired under warranty. Bob Evans has always had a way of getting people to do what he wants, usually without the unsuspecting victims even knowing it and amazingly, he also convinced the driver to fill up his empty bed with a load of drums. Both trucks were stacked perilously full as they set off for New Orleans just before dark.

It was a miserable night and the rain came down in sheets. Without windshield wipers, Bob was forced to steer his towed truck with his head out the window. As the lead truck sloshed through one puddle after another Bob would receive a face full of water each time. He had warned the other driver that there was a low overpass near Pineville, about halfway to New Orleans. The driver assured him that he would stop to make sure that the two heavily loaded trucks would clear the low bridge before pressing on.

They reached Pineville in the middle of the night and of course, the weary driver forgot about the bridge. By the time he remembered and slammed on his his brakes it was too late. CRASH! the drums in the first truck made a horrible noise as they smashed into the concrete barrier and then careened down onto Bob's truck. SMASH! the drums piled high in Bob's truck hit the bridge next. It was literally raining drums and they were scattered all about. Luckily no one was injured but the Chief of the Pineville Police department was not amused. He wanted to know who was going to pay for the damage to the concrete overpass! Bob told the police officer to send him the bill. After collecting what drums they could, they finally limped into New Orleans the next day. It was the last business trip Bob ever made with his father.

Slowly, almost painfully, the Evans Cooperage Company began to grow. Bob and his brothers scoured New Orleans and surrounding areas with a couple of small trucks looking for used drums to recondition and resell. As previously mentioned, wooden barrels were no longer an important part of the business and gradually Bob purchased inexpensive, second-hand machinery to hasten the reconditioning of steel drums. Still, sheer hard work could only go so far, the future prospects for the small company were dim because the process of collecting drums was woefully inefficient. There simply had to be a better way.

Simple ideas can be revolutionary while complicated ideas rarely change anything. Bob Evans realized that he just could not haul enough drums with a standard truck trailer to make much money reconditioning drums. So he decided to build a bigger truck. He traded in his car for the down payment on a cab forward truck. With the help of a local blacksmith who had a hand drill press, and a rear axle he purchased at a scrap yard, Bob created the largest trailer the law allowed. Although it was bolted together instead of riveted and was almost overly simple in design, it was big. In fact, suddenly Bob Evans had one of the largest trailers in the country. In one fell swoop he had increased the number of drums he could haul from 180 to 220, he had instantly upped his capacity on each run by more that 20%!

The largest manufacturer of drums in New Orleans in the late 30's was Wilson and Bennett Company which would later be absorbed by Inland Steel. Bob was hard to miss in his big rig and soon the plant manager asked him if he could haul drums for Wilson and Bennett during their peak periods. These were boom days for the drum business. Huge amounts of lubricating oils and solvents were being shipped overseas from the Port of New Orleans to keep up with the demands of man's insatiable appetite for waging war. Just as the Spanish Civil War was finally winding down Mussolini mustered up his courage and invaded Ethiopia. While the European powers were warily eying each other and preparing for inevitable conflict, Japan was quietly importing enormous amounts of lube oil for its war machine. Fifty-five gallon drums made in New Orleans were inadvertently carrying the fuels that would soon plunge a world into war.

Bob Evans was not about to miss out on this boom period and by borrowing every cent he could and by scrounging around scrap yards he built more trailers. Soon all four brothers had a large truck and quickly Evans Cooperage Company was becoming less of a reconditioner and more of a trucking company. But it was grueling work and frequently the Evans boys would put in 24 hour shifts. Bob drove all night so that he could manage the business by day. Although he was making money, he began to resent the fact that he was hauling other company's drums. When he amassed $2,500 he bought a small reconditioning plant on the outskirts of New Orleans, his first real plant and the first of many plants he would own in his life time. With a plant of his own he felt like he finally had a business that was going somewhere.

Bob Evans is a demanding employer but he never asks somebody to do something that he is not willing to do himself. Still, he has no tolerance for slackers and soon a family feud was brewing. It seems Bob's younger brother Buddy would occasionally shirk his driving duties and park his truck for the night and make his way to a party or dance. The next morning Bob would have to explain to the Wilson and Bennett Plant Manager why the load had not been delivered on time. Bob and Buddy were destined for a clash, or more like an epic collision, for it was Buddy who had robbed Bob's box those many years ago and Bob never forgot it. It's safe to say that they didn't get along very well.

Bob Evans is not by nature a patient man and after repeatedly trying to convince his younger brother to bear up to his responsibility, he exploded. He called his three brothers; Buddy, Nuppy and Richard, in for a meeting. With a flare for the dramatic, he explained Buddy's exploits, which of course they already knew and then told them that he was walking out of the room and that they were going to decide who was going to stay, Buddy or Bob, but not both. He would come back in an hour. If they elected to keep Buddy in the company they could have the business and Bob would walk away for good. The brothers knew Bob well enough to know this was not an idle threat.

An hour later when Bob returned Buddy was gone, the brothers had made their choice. When you distill business acumen down to the raw basics, it consists mainly of having the guts to make difficult decisions. In a family business, the decisions become even tougher.

The war time boom proved bitter sweet. Ironically, just as the Evans Cooperage Company really started to prosper, Bob was drafted. The same market place that needed all those 55 gallon steel drums now needed Bob Evans.

CHAPTER THREE

INTERLUDES AND INTRIGUES

Many people remember exactly where they were, what they were doing, even what they were wearing, when they heard the epochal news on December 7, 1941. Bob Evans does not. It is a safe bet though that as Japanese airplanes were laying waste to the U.S. Pacific Fleet in Pearl Harbor, Bob Evans was either driving a truck loaded with Wilson and Bennett drums destined for the Port of New Orleans or sitting behind his desk trying to figure a way to locate more used drums for his fledgling reconditioning plant. Like everyone else in New Orleans, Bob was stunned by the news of the attack and the subsequent declarations of war. However, he was nearly 30 years old and his business was just starting to blossom, the reality of war didn't hit him until it became obvious that like most men in America under the age of 30, he would be drafted. His business, which now consisted of ten large trucks, a small reconditioning plant and twenty full time employees, a business that he had toiled at without a break for nearly four years, would be left floundering.

Anticipating the obvious he went to the draft board and asked for a three to six month deferment. "What for?" the enlistment officer inquired. "To prepare my business for my absence," Bob explained hopefully. "I don't have anybody to run it and I need time to find somebody who can. You must understand that I can't just walk away, I've spent the last fours years working every day to build this business."

The harried officer had no sympathy. "Sorry, I have heard that one before. This is war, son. What would happen if you died on the battlefield, who would run your business then?" This struck Bob as a stupid question but it did impress upon him that this war stuff was indeed serious business. Bob saw the writing on the wall and resigned himself to the fact that he would soon be drafted and the business would have to survive without him.

Bob's brother Nuppy was also drafted leaving the business in Richard's twenty year old, inexperienced hands. Bob hastily persuaded his sister Leoni to give up her job at Popovich's department store downtown and join the firm to help his youngest brother manage the business before he shipped out to Riverside, California for basic training. Despite his lack of a college degree, Bob thought his management experience would qualify him for Officer Candidate School. He was bitterly disappointed when the Army thought otherwise. When basic training was complete he was shipped east to Camp Kilmer, New Jersey as an enlisted man, one of thousands of buck privates awaiting posting overseas.

Bob was eventually herded aboard a Liberty ship and along with thousands of other anxious and often sea sick young men, made the long passage across the Atlantic to North Africa. In early 1943, Rommel, the Nazi General, known as the Desert Fox, was already in retreat and Bob and his battalion were soon part of the human wave that invaded Sicily. After beating back the Nazis they dug in and fortified the beach head in anticipation of the second line of Germany's assault. They prepared for an invasion that never came. Bob recalls that he spent most of his time in a vineyard eating grapes, reading books and thinking about his business back home. The biggest thrill of the so called invasion was encountering a group of Italian soldiers positively ecstatic to be taken prisoner by the Americans.

After he had been turned down for OCS, Bob lost his ambition, the war was just a major inconvenience in his life, something to be endured, until he could return to New Orleans and his business. He spent a lot of time worrying about the business and thinking of ways to expand it when he returned. In fact, his nickname was 'horizontal' because he was often laying in his bunk or hammock and staring off into space. Bob Evans' mind is rarely at rest however and it was while lying in his hammock that he conjured up an image of a rotary washer for drums. And not only did Bob build the washer when he returned, an updated version of it is still in use in the reconditioning plant today.

It is hard to imagine Bob Evans, the consummate man of action, taking such a passive role. But the Army didn't recognize or need his talent, to them he was just another grunt, another number in the ultimate number's game. As a foot soldier it is nearly impossible to grasp the big picture of war, politics and strategy. You feel like a pawn on a chess board and your only desire is for the game to be over. As the war dragged on Bob realized that the fastest way out of the Army was to take calculated risks and volunteer for combat missions. You compiled points after so many missions (if you happened to be in the right campaigns) and then, if you were still alive and you had earned enough points, you were rotated out of the service. Bob manned a 90mm anti-aircraft gun as he and his battalion followed General Mark Clark's forces up the Italian peninsula. To the annoyance of his Commanding Officer, who didn't want to lose another good man, he volunteered for every combat mission available. Bob Evans has never been afraid to take risks and they usually pay off.

One day, with his company bogged down in a muddy camp somewhere in the Italian countryside, Bob came across a form that was an application for a 60 day leave of absence. Figuring he had nothing to lose he filled out the form and filed it with the proper authorities. His mates laughed at him, convinced that he was dreaming and just wasting his time. "There's Bob Evans, playing every angle," they chided him. They stopped laughing a couple weeks later when Bob received an urgent message advising him to get ready for an extended leave. Because of his extensive combat experience his request had been granted. He was on his way back to the States.

He flew in a B-26, a twin engine bomber that was forced to take the long way home because it could not carry enough fuel for a direct crossing of the Atlantic. When he finally arrived in New Orleans he was relieved to see that Evans Cooperage was still afloat, although they were just clinging to life, eeking out an existence reconditioning drums that were bound overseas. Leoni had taken a very proprietary interest in the business and was reluctant to share information with her big brother. She kept her older brother at arms length throughout his leave and Bob knew that it was pointless to force the issue with her because he would soon be back in uniform and he needed her to continue to manage the business. Uncharacteristically, (doling out compliments has never been easy for Bob) he told Leoni and Richard too, that they were doing a great job and offered encouragement instead of advice.

It was a frustrating visit because it was obvious to Bob that there was a lot of money to be made out of the war effort but his brother and sister were not realizing the potential. He made a mental note that when he returned after the war, he would have to figure out a diplomatic way to wrest control of the company back from his sister. He also spent considerable time with his mother during his leave and assured her (for 'Robby' as she called him, was the apple of her eye) that he would stop volunteering for combat missions when he returned. However, when his leave ended the Army reassigned him to Ft. Knox in Kentucky. He was assigned to a tank division and he was still in Kentucky when the war finally ended in 1945.

Bob arrived back in New Orleans for good in June 1945 and stepping off the train at Union Station he received the tumultuous greeting that awaited all returning soldiers. However, the euphoria faded quickly and that was fine with Bob Evans. Despite the fact that he was decorated with several battle stars he was only too ready to put the war time interlude behind him. Bob Evans saw little that was glorious or worth repeating of his war time service, he was not the kind of man to relive the war over and over. The war, while necessary, was a combination of inexorable boredom and fleeting moments of madness when you realized that one of your rounds might have just sent a pilot to his doom. Bob was ready to forget the war. It was time to get on with his life and for Bob Evans, life and business were not easily separated.

His sister suspected that Bob would try to take the reigns of the business and she resented him for it. "I suppose you are thinking about taking over again," she asked him defensively on his first day back at the office. "No," he responded in a quiet but undeniably firm voice, "I'm not thinking about it, I'm doing it." And that was that, so much for diplomacy, Bob Evans was back at the helm of Evans Cooperage Company and there he would remain for the next 48 years.

The Port of New Orleans continued to boom after the war. The enormous enterprise to rebuild Europe and Asia was meted out in 55 gallon drums and New Orleans was the drum capital of the world. Bob knew that the quickest way to expand his business was to establish a filling operation. If he had the ability to fill drums, he would in essence become his own customer and have a much greater control of his sales revenues. Evans Cooperage could receive petroleums and other products in bulk and fill their own reconditioned drums. It was a classic Bob Evans strategy, wonderfully simple yet unique to the industry.

There was only one problem with the strategy. Evans Cooperage didn't have the money required to expand, especially in the fashion Bob envisioned. Fate intervened when a local business broker came calling. It seemed the broker was representing a client from Chicago, a former partner of Acme Barrel, a large drum reconditioner who wanted to operate his own company in New Orleans. The client, Ben Uttal was enchanted by New Orleans, the food, the jazz, the ambience, and Bob's little plant in Jefferson Parish was just what he wanted. Bob sold him the company for $40,000 which was a lot of money in 1946. Uttal agreed to fulfill certain contracts, including a large order with Pan American Oil, one of the largest refineries in New Orleans and Bob agreed to a no compete clause on any reconditioning business within the state of Louisiana. Bob did reserve the right to recondition drums for his soon to be launched filling business.

Although he had just sold his plant, Bob Evans was certainly not planning to stay out of the drum business for long. Convinced that filling was the key, he bought a large parcel of property on the Intracoastal Canal, known locally as the Harvey Canal, and began to sketch out the plans for a new reconditioning plant. Like building bigger trucks in the late 30's, moving onto the water in the late 40's would prove to be a master stroke. However, there were several unexpected obstacles to overcome before a single drum would be reconditioned in the new plant.

The first problem reared its head when Bob was contacted by the Purchasing Agent of Pan American Oil. It seems Ben Uttal was reneging on a large contract, claiming that the profit margin was too thin. This infuriated

Bob who confronted Uttal on the allegation. "All Purchasing Agents are whores," Uttal informed Bob. "I can't make any money on that contract." Bob, in a fit of spontaneous rage declared, "if you don't fill the order for drums than I'll buy them from you myself and fill the order." "You'll lose nothing but money," Uttal chortled, "and when the dust settles I'll go in and get the business at the price I want."

Bob Evans is driven by a powerful mixture of honor and vindictiveness. If he gives you his word, you can take that word to the bank. But if you deceive him intentionally, God help you, he will come after you. Bob Evans has a profound sense of right and wrong and an obsession with righting what he perceives to be wrongs. Bob managed to fill the order for Pan American, losing money on every drum and having to suffer the indignity of buying the drums from his old plant at an inflated price. However he was comforted by the knowledge that he would one day get even with Ben Uttal, there was absolutely no doubt in his mind.

Although Bob Evans had no formal engineering training he has a remarkable ability to apply creative solutions to practical problems. He has never been burdened by conventional wisdom. Indeed, his lack of formal education probably inspired his imagination, for he is more of an inventor than an engineer and as his business grew and the processes became more complex he always seemed to figure out an ingenious and often times unorthodox method of accomplishing a mechanical task. He also had gall. When it came time to design the new plant and wharf, he hired a young engineering apprentice and the two of them went to work.

Unfortunately, Bob's dear friend, banker and in many ways his mentor, Tom Nicholson, President of First National Bank of Jefferson Parrish, along with other bankers Bob approached for financing, insisted that Bob hire a large engineering firm to design the plant and a major contracting company to build it. Bob's instincts told him this was the wrong approach but when you borrow money you don't have a lot of power. Bob Evans always had the ability to borrow money, he has always inspired confidence in financial people. Tom Nicholson kidded him for years, "Bob, you have the ability to borrow more money than you need and that's not good for you."

When the plant was finally finished in 1947 the cost overruns totaled $40,000, a colossal figure in those days and Bob moved into his brand new facility absolutely broke. The so-called experts had put him in a big financial hole although he did have a fine new reconditioning plant and filling facility.

Eventually orders started to come in and the second coming of Evans Cooperage Company was off and running. Being on the water was a great competitive advantage. Evans could receive barge loads of lubricating and cooking oils directly, without a transportation middleman, fill his own reconditioned drums and send them on to waiting ships by barge. As Evans began to prosper Bob never forgot his pledge to get even with Ben Uttal. A large cache of government drums stored in Shreveport proved to be Bob's opportunity for revenge.

When the Federal authorities decided to sell the drums they sent out requests for bids. Ben Uttal made a rather low bid for the more than 40,000 drums but he was confident he would get them anyway because he had very little competition in the state. What he didn't expect was that Bob Evans would also bid on the drums. Bob's bid was higher and the government sold him the drums. Uttal was furious and charged Bob with violating his no compete agreement. "Ben," Bob informed him smugly when Uttal called to protest, "these drums have nothing to do with Louisiana, I am buying them from the United States Government. They are sitting on U.S. Government property, not state of Louisiana property and I am sending my check to Washington D.C." Needless to say Uttal was enraged and sued Bob and

Evans Cooperage. Even Bob's lawyer was nervous about the case, "it can go either way," he told Bob. When the verdict was read Ben Uttal had lost the case and with it, his spirit. Uttal had been mismanaging the company for several of years and soon after the case was lost, he went bankrupt. The coup de grace came when Bob bought back his old plant at auction for a fraction of what he had sold it for.

These were busy but heady days for Bob Evans. He was in his mid thirties, robust and full of vigor. He was passionate about his business and for the first time in his life realized that he just might build a major company after all, the backyard cooperage seem far astern. Five feet, ten inches tall, powerfully built with wavy hair and a gleam in his eye, Bob Evans had a sense of presence. You noticed him when he walked into a crowded room. He often made his way across the river into the French Quarter after work. It was on one of these forays that he and a friend stopped off for a drink in the lounge of the elegant Roosevelt Hotel (now the Fairmont) on Barone Street. He didn't know it then but the lovely young woman sitting with her girlfriend at a nearby table would change his life forever.

With typical audacity Bob introduced himself and his friend. Janice Roberts was intrigued with the confident young man standing before her. He was different than most men she met after the war. He was not confused about where his life was going. And she could tell he was obviously smitten with her. Before the night was out she accepted his offer for a future date. This was the beginning of a six year relationship that would culminate in marriage in 1952.

Janice was from the tiny town of Downsville in northern Louisiana not far from Monroe. Born and raised on a small cotton farm she had come to New Orleans during the war. Like most young women, Janice learned a trade and contributed to the war effort. She became a welder and worked in the Naval

Shipyard. It is hard to imagine this beautiful women standing over a glowing electrode while perched high on the scaffold joining steel plates on the topsides of a ship, but war time demands sacrifices from everyone. By all accounts Janice was a first class welder too. Janice was an independent woman, especially for her times. After the war Janice decided to stay in New Orleans and went to work at Solari's. This unique beanery in the heart of the Quarter had a large lunch counter and also was a gourmet delicatessen on the corner of Royal and Iberville. Bob often stopped in for lunch and although he claims that it was just because the food was good, it might also have had something to do with a certain employee. After a year's stint at Solari's, Janice took a job as an inventory clerk in an office at Lederlee Laboratories and there she worked during Bob's long but steady courtship.

In many ways the steel drum industry directly reflects America's foreign trade policy. A close look at the ups and downs of the drum business gives insights into who is receiving what from the U.S. Government and U. S. companies. Drums and their contents are a window of sorts, offering a glimpse into the world of international commerce. With the Marshall Plan already in full swing, a new threat, the emergence of Russia as a major obstacle to a shaky European peace accord, created a huge market for liquid asphalt. Why asphalt? Because asphalt is used to build runways and defense fortifications. How is asphalt shipped to Europe? In 55 gallon steel drums of course.

Bob Evans could smell the boom in asphalt but he couldn't taste it. He watched in frustration as a few of his filling customers did a landmark business by purchasing large amounts of asphalt from refineries, including American Liberty in Mt. Pleasant, Texas and Pan American Refinery in New Orleans (the refineries did the filling, in mostly reconditioned drums, themselves) and shipped it over-seas at inflated prices. Bob wanted desperately to be a part of this loop and he came up with an imaginative way to do just that.

Bob found a refinery in Big Spring, Texas that produced tremendous amounts of asphalt as a by-product and convinced them to sell it to him at a very low price. He then charmed the local railroad company into giving him a ridiculously low tariff based on the huge amount of asphalt he promised to ship. Finally, he offered asphalt brokers these incredibly cheap rates if they agreed to have Evans Cooperage fill their drums. The results were astounding, in short order Evans Cooperage became the major asphalt filler in New Orleans and Pan American and American Liberty were all but shut out of the asphalt market. There was one big problem however, the orders were coming in so rapidly that Evans Cooperage did not have nearly enough drums to meet the demand.

"The reason Bob Evans was a success," says Mildred Pourciau without any doubt in her voice, "is because he could make things happen." Mildred who worked with Bob for 40 years and ended up managing the filling business was one of the few employees who could tell Bob that she didn't like what he was doing and get away with it. He respected her opinions dearly. "In business there are two kinds of people," Mildred continued, "people who talk about things and people who make things happen. Bob's problem was that he made too much happen. I'll never forget the crazy time when we had to find all those drums."

Bob placed an urgent advertisement in National Barrel & Drum Association Newsletter offering to buy low grade drums. There was at the time, a surplus of drums in the Midwest and Bob was hopeful of not only finding the nearly 50,000 drums he needed but also of being able to buy them on credit. Bob has never been daunted by a lack of money and he was prepared to sign over a portion of the filling contract if it came to that.

Bob's quest took him first to St. Louis, where a local reconditioner had offered drums at a low price but was skeptical of Bob's creative financing schemes. While in St. Louis Bob met with officials of the Federal Barge Line, one of the largest haulers on the Mississippi River and her tributaries. By studying the tariff closely, Bob realized that steel and its by-products had a very low rate. Consequently, if Bob could make the barge line officials apply that tariff to drums, he could literally ship drums from any northern river port all the way to New Orleans cheaper than he could transport them across the city by truck. Bob decided to continue his search in Chicago.

Trilla Cooperage was one of the largest reconditioners in the Chicago area and Bob set up an appointment immediately upon his arrival. Bob was escorted into the inner sanctum, there was something mysterious about the Trilla offices which of course contributed to the completely unfounded rumor that would later surface that Trilla was a mob outfit. Lester Trilla was a strikingly handsome man with dark features and bright, intense eyes. Bob was taken aback by his first impression of this passionate man. Trilla had the ability to make you feel like you were the most important person in the world, he gave you his undivided attention. Bob certainly had a style of his own and Trilla was equally impressed with Bob's forthrightness. He laid out his proposition without pomp and circumstance. Trilla liked the feel of the deal. "Okay Bob, I'll give you the drums and you pay me when you get paid, I don't need to be part of your filling contract, that just complicates the deal." That was it with a simple handshake and a mutual trust, Bob and Lester Trilla sealed the deal and more importantly, launched what would become a life long friendship and business relationship.

Even Lester Trilla had to scramble to find 50,000 drums but he didn't want to give Bob that impression. During negotiations he had made it sound like all he needed to do was to place a call to the plant and presto, the drums would be ready. Lester went to work calling every reconditioner in Chicago, while his brother took Bob to an afternoon Cub's game at Wrigley Field. Some how Trilla found the drums and loaded them onto waiting barges. When Bob finally pointed his Cadillac south he could rest easy, his precious drums were not far behind.

It was in the asphalt business where Bob's decision to move his plant to the waterfront really paid off. After working day and night to fill those initial orders his business blossomed. Bob was able to bring in both asphalt and drums by barge and therefore he consistently priced his competitors out of the market

As 1952 was winding down Bob decided that the time was right. He was 40 years old and for the first time in his life felt he had achieved some degree of financial stability. On Christmas Eve he finally proposed to Janice. When she accepted his offer of marriage she didn't realize that she would have to rush their wedding preparations. "You see Janice," Bob explained, "If we get married before the end of the year, I'll save $1,100 on income taxes!"

A ROBERT EVANS ALBUM

Robert Evans standing beside his brother Charles (Buddy), 1915

Evans Cooperage Inc. shortly after moving to site on the Harvey Canal

Robert and Janice Evans, 1955

Janice Evans, 1955

Robert and Janice Evans with their daughter, Jan Hamilton

Janice Evans, 1996

The Evans Family

Robert Evans and his Grandchildren

Robert and Ronald Evans

Janice and Robert Evans at Home in Gretna

Gary Hamilton, Robert Evans, Ronald Evans and Jan Hamilton

Robert Evans and Gary Hamilton

Robert Evans and John Anderson

Bena Saucier

Mildred Pourciau

Jimmy Richoux

Robert Evans and Ty Techera

Gary Roerig

Valentine Emery

Elliot Arendt

Pablo Maique

Horace Williams

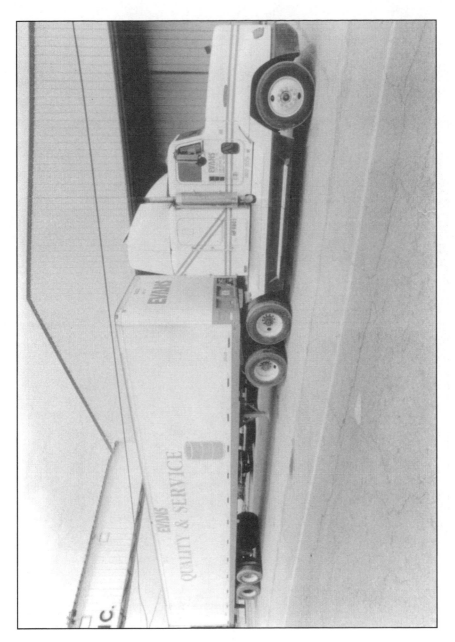

An Evans Trademark Truck

Jay Horman

John Anderson and Kathy Thibodaux

Ronald J. Evans

CHAPTER FOUR

GIANT SLAYER

Mr. and Mrs. Evans spent their honeymoon in Chicago and rang in the new year with the Trilla family at the elegant Edgewater Hotel on Lake Shore Drive. The future seemed bright indeed as they held each other close and danced into the next year serenaded by the crooning of a youthful Sinatra. Lester Trilla, who was famous for his hospitality, had shown the new couple a marvelous time in the Windy City. Bob and Lester Trilla were becoming fast friends and their personal and business relationship would prove profitable for both and weather many hurdles during a span of more than 25 years. In fact shortly after the wedding Trilla invested in Evans cooperage and remained valuable but minor stockholder until just before his death when Bob offered him a generous buy out.

Back home again and ever frugal, Bob and Janice moved in with Bob's mother to save money. Two years later, Janice was pregnant. Bob was surprised how excited he was at the prospect of becoming a father and he asked Janice to give up her job as an inventory clerk at Lederle Laboratories, a position she had held for six years. When Bob told Mildred Pourciau that Janice was expecting, typically she cut straight to the point. "At your age, you better have them two at a time, you are almost too old for kids now."

Mildred's premonition was almost eerie, for when Janice delivered in December of 1954, she had twins. Little Ronnie and Robbie added a new, unexpected dimension to Bob Evans' life. When you have children later in life you seem to appreciate them more and this was certainly the case with Bob. He'd been saddled with responsibility for so long that he had not planned on having children of his own, in some ways he felt like he had already raised one family. But Bob became a devoted and not surprisingly, demanding father. His twin sons were followed two years later by a daughter, Jan who became the apple of her father's eye and two years later by another son, Jeffrey. Bob worshipped his young family. Business and family, these were the pervading passions in Bob's life. He had few other interests.

The same year the twins were born Evans Cooperage decided to manufacture new drums. The decision was wrought innocently enough, if he built his own drums he could control his filling business much more efficiently. Bob Evans has always wanted to control his own destiny, at times to a fault and he never intended to become a major manufacturer of steel drums, he just didn't want to have to rely on other drum builders when he had a large order to fill.

The first new drum plant was put together hastily, in bits and pieces. Bob was anxious to start manufacturing but he didn't have the capital to build a proper plant and he was not about to repeat the expensive cost overruns of the reconditioning plant. From the beginning Evans had difficulty finding a supplier of steel. Bob personally contacted four major steel companies, U.S. Steel, Republic Steel, Inland Steel and Jones & Laughlin Steel. Bob chose these companies specifically because he thought they would offer price advantages. U.S. and Republic had mills in the nearby Birmingham, Alabama area and steel could be shipped inexpensively to New Orleans by barge, train or truck. Inland and Jones & Laughlin had local drum plants and moved a lot of steel by barge from Chicago and Pittsburgh to New Orleans. And while Bob realized that all of these companies also built drums and that the New Orleans market was already saturated with drum plants, it never dawned on him that they would gang up against a tiny company like Evans. He didn't realize it at the time but these first innocent attempts to buy steel for his fledging plant were the initial volleys of what would eventually become his own private war with the American steel industry.

In the steel industry's defense, there was a general shortage of steel in the 1950's. Nobody anticipated the overwhelming, decade long demand for steel. Domestically, the country was in the midst of an enormous building boom, including Eisenhower's epic Interstate Highway program and internationally, the Marshall Plan and general rebuilding of Europe and Asia required massive quantities of American steel until their own new mills could be completed.

Finally, Bob located a local warehouse that needed sheet steel and they shared a pool barge from the parent company's mill in St. Louis after Bob explained how this arrangement would save them both money. Gradually the Evans new drum plant worked out the bugs in the manufacturing process and steadily increased capacity. Bob Evans loved manufacturing right from the start. With his innovative approach to engineering and problem solving Bob was made for manufacturing and this soon became his preferred aspect of the business. Although he had no formal engineering training, Bob's plants always included fresh ideas and his industry peers often stopped by New Orleans for a taste of Cajun cooking and a look at how Bob Evans had tackled a particularly thorny manufacturing problem. However, the first couple of years new drum production remained limited to containers used exclusively for Evans' filling operation.

This would change however when one sun drenched autumn day in 1957, a tall visitor with a Texas drawl arrived unannounced in Bob's office. The man introduced himself as the manager of a large independent tank terminal in Houston which was filling vast amounts of vegetable oil in drums for export. The mysterious visitor explained that they were moving their vegetable oil filling business to a recently purchased terminal in New Orleans, not far from the Evans plant. The man, obviously exploring where Bob's comfort zone was in the strict hierarchy of new drum manufacturing in New Orleans, first poised the question hypothetically, "was Evans Cooperage interested in supplying new drums for this operation, a lot of new drums?"

Bob immediately realized that he was being put in a predicament. The market structure in New Orleans for new drums was well established and while some people, including Bob Evans, might have seen this as a form of price fixing, the consistency of the market seemed to satisfy both suppliers and users and Bob knew he did not have the clout to tamper with it. As much as Bob relished the possibility of a major order for new drums, he was not prepared to upset the market structure by offering a discounted price for drums which is what Bob was sure the man was after. Why else would he approach Evans if it was not to achieve a better priced drum?

However, the terminal representative was not fishing for a price concession, indeed, they had purchased 300,000 steel drums the year before in Houston at list price and anticipated purchasing a similar amount in New Orleans. No doubt Bob's eyes widened significantly at this point in the conversation. An order of that magnitude would make Evans a player in the new drum business overnight.

The reason the terminal operation was considering Evans had nothing to do with price, it was a logistical consideration that once again highlighted Bob Evans' foresight. Evans was the only drum manufacturer in New Orleans located on the water. New drums could be loaded directly onto barges, towed to the terminal for filling and delivered directly to waiting ships, thus eliminating the need to truck drums to a loading dock. Bob's decision to locate on the Harvey Canal had proved to be a master stroke.

"Here is the tough part," the mysterious visitor said with a coy smile, "we need 90,000 drums six weeks from now." Bob groaned, sat back in his chair and after a long period of silence told the man in his typically forthright way, "then I can't accept the order. While I believe that if we worked in shifts around the clock, seven days a week, we probably could meet the order, you and I both know there will be delays and I can't accept the responsibility for slowing down your operation. I just can't leave you exposed." Whereas most people would have bit their tongue and quietly accepted the order and then probably fail to meet it, Bob's candor impressed the visitor mightily. "They told me you were honest and they were right. All I want from you is your commitment that you will do your best to meet the order and I'll take responsibility for delays beyond your control." A commitment was something Bob was prepared to give and it was as good as gold. Bob shook the man's hand and before the door closed behind him he was on the phone to his brother Richard, the plant manager. There was work to be done and no time to be lost.

The mysterious visitor was a man named McCullum, who ran Hess Terminals. David McCullum later went on to become President of Amerada Hess, a major oil company and was the right hand man of principle owner, Leon Hess. Hess was a real maverick in the oil business, which is saying something because you must to be a maverick by definition just to be in the oil business. Whether they were mavericks risking their companies with every decision or just executive decision makers and purchasing agents, decisive managers of every ilk invariably found that dealing with Bob Evans was a stark and refreshing contrast to dealing with the bureaucracy laden drum plants owned by major steel mills. Bob made decisions and he made them fast. The next month was probably the most hectic time in the history of Evans Cooperage. The small plant was simply not prepared to meet an order of this magnitude. Bob immediately purchased new equipment and many new. people were hired, trained, fired when they could not keep up with the frantic pace and additional workers then had to be hired and retrained. To complicate matters the swedger, the flanger and the seam welder, machinery vital to the operation of making new drums, all broke down from being overloaded and had to constantly be coaxed back into action. One can just imagine the metallic roar as 3,000, 18 gauge, 55 gallon steel drums a day rolled off the overburdened line. Amazingly Evans fulfilled the order, delivering the last barge load just before midnight on the eve of the contract deadline. This event foreshadowed what would eventually become an Evans company trademark, when the job required it, every available resource would be deployed to meet the job. The entire work force pitches in and although at times the long hours become excruciating, the substantial paydays at the end of the week make all the work worthwhile.

When the dust settled and the noise level returned to a manageable din, Bob tallied up the results. In just over a month Evans had earned $125,000, an amount that was more than the plant had cost to build! One month of work paid for the new plant, maybe there was something to this new drum manufacturing after all. Of course, one of the primary reasons the profits were so substantial was because drums were selling at inflated prices established by the major American steel firms.

Buoyed by additional orders from Hess, Bob immediately made plans to develop a faster line. Handling much of the design work himself and utilizing in-house engineers and crafty second-hand purchases, by 1960, Evans Cooperage had a new high speed line, featuring a unique single line conveyor that could produce 600 drums an hour. This line, which was one of the fastest new drum lines in the world, marked Evans' entry into big time manufacturing. It also marked the beginning of a bitter battle between Bob Evans and several major American steel companies.

Clearly Evans' big contract launched an unprecedented price war in the local new drum market. For many years the set price of a drum had remained fixed at $6.87. However, within months of Evans receiving their large order, one of the local drum plants owned by a large out of town steel company, dropped the price of a drum by 27 cents. This triggered further price reductions by the other large steel companies. In fact, ten years later, in 1967, the price of a new drum had fallen to $5.75, which was nearly equal to the cost of the raw steel required to build the drum. How could the drum industry survive in such a cut throat market? It survived by employing a two tier market structure based on the illegal practice of reciprocity.

The one facet of business that Bob Evans detests more than anything else, is when healthy competition falls victim to unfair trade practices. From intrusive governmental controls to monopolies to price fixing, Bob Evans always fought for a level playing field. He believed fervently in the symmetry and honesty of the natural market place. In the New Orleans steel and drum market of the late 50's, 60's and early 70's, however, the playing field was anything but level, illegal reciprocity was rampant. Bob was convinced that drum divisions of several big steel companies were maneuvering to put him and other small operators out of business, or at least out of the new drum market. If this were the case, and the evidence surely supports it, then these executives severely underestimated the tenacity and resourcefulness of their foe.

Reciprocity is, of course, a natural progression of any relationship. If I agree to buy your products, then you agree to buy mine. It is wide spread in every type of buying and selling situation. Why then is the practice of reciprocity generally illegal? Because reciprocity is easy to abuse, especially in an industry dominated by a few large companies with enormous purchasing power. Bob Evans, in a series of episodes written in 1977 and in an highly unorthodox move sent out to all of Evans' important customers, describes two varying degrees of reciprocity, the abuse and the perversion. These thoughtful, emotionally charged episodes are reproduced in their original form in the appendix. They represent a unique and honest look at both Bob's personal battles and the overall state of malaise and general demise of the American steel industry during the long period of suffering in the 1960's and 70's. What makes these episodes so intriguing is that although they were written in the mid 70's, they accurately predicted the collapse of the domestic steel industry and the continued increase in the use of foreign steel by U.S. manufacturers.

The abuse of reciprocity occurs when you can control prices of one product or service based upon the purchase of an entirely different product or service. In the New Orleans drum market in the 1960's, the large steel companies with drum divisions purchased huge amounts of fuel, lubricants and chemicals, products often filled and shipped in drums and therefore could insist on channeling container business to their own drum plants. It is simple, if we buy X amount of lubricating oil from you at this price, then you have to buy X amount of our drums at this price. In very restrictive markets, like New Orleans, this practice makes it very difficult for newcomers to claw their way into the market. Decisions are based more on reciprocity or buying power than on price and service as defined by the market place.

While this may sound like typical small company sour grapes, it can be forcefully argued that the practice of reciprocity was a major contributor to the decline of heavy industry, particularly the steel industry, (and to a lesser degree, the auto industry) in America. After years of controlling markets based solely on their purchasing power instead of the quality and price of their products and services, they were suddenly faced with well capitalized foreign competition. They had lost their competitive edge and were ripe for plunder. Reciprocity makes companies lose touch with the market place. When you can command market share regardless of your product quality, quality suffers. Indeed, the entire corporate downsizing trend of today is an attempt not to be lulled into the complacency to which the practice of reciprocity contributed. The mood of business today is to stay lean, trim and attuned to every whim of the market place. The New Orleans drum market represents a vivid portrait, albeit a microcosm, of why the American steel industry collapsed so dramatically in the early 80's and has never fully recovered.

The perversion of reciprocity occurs when the practice is used to destroy competition. Bob Evans is convinced that the pricing practices of big steel companies in the 1960's and into the 1970's were designed to drive him, and other smaller companies out of the New Orleans new drum market. Specifically, one major steel company kept driving the price down on accounts that were not governed by reciprocity. This drum company owned by a major steel mill was able to drive the price so low that it eventually cost more to buy the steel necessary to build the drum than what the finished drum sold for in these non reciprocity driven markets, that is, of course. when steel was available at all.

Bob Evans was never a man to despair and while he might have railed to anyone who would listen that the world was conspiring against him, that he was fighting against incredible odds, in many ways he was made for a fight like this. He had ironclad strength in his convictions, he never wavered from a position he believed just and he was fiercely competitive. The game of business for Bob Evans was never solely or even primarily about attaining personal wealth, it was much grander than that. It was a great personal challenge, to build a company, design new equipment, tackle new markets, take on competitors, Bob Evans relished the battles and his victories were hard won.

A typical day in 1960 would see Bob Evans arrive in his office before 8:00 AM. He would be dressed in a light linen suit with two tone black and white shoes. By 10:00 AM the jacket would be off and the tie loosened. He would spend hours on the phone. He consulted with Lester Trilla often and urged Trilla to get into new drum manufacturing, a move Trilla resisted but later consented to, a decision that helped his company immensely. He often spoke with Frank Langella, who owned and operated Bayonne Barrel & Drum a reconditioning plant in Newark, New Jersey. Langella was a technical innovator and admired by everyone in the industry. As long time Vice President Jimmy Richoux puts it, "Bob was the master of his own three ring circus, new drums, reconditioned drums and filling. There was never any question who was in charge." He never forgot his roots in reconditioning and trucking and Evans trademark trucks continued to get bigger and bigger and reached out all over the south to collect used drums.

Bob Evans spent over half his day in the plants. He had a natural "walkabout" managerial style. His keen, and often critical eye, followed drums down the line and he was always looking for ways to improve production. He would often return to the office and immediately sketch a rough design for a new piece of equipment. Without realizing it, he was emulating Japanese engineers and managers long before it was trendy to do so and not surprisingly he would come to admire the Japanese greatly in the upcoming decades. In fact, as he traded more and more with the Japanese he gradually realized that they had the potential to be manufacturing heavyweights. More than once he warned executives of large American steel firms to watch out for their Japanese competitors but his warnings fell on deaf ears. Bob Evans, who was one of the first U.S. manufacturers to purchase Japanese steel, saw a sleeping giant awakening and when the Japanese revolution came he not only wasn't hurt by it, he profited by it.

Another reason Bob Evans spent so much time in the plant was that he truly loved the manufacturing process. It was pure and it was honest. If you designed better equipment, it translated into better drums, which ultimately led to more satisfied customers and a better bottom line. Bob Evans believed in this simplistic rule of business deep in his soul and while it ultimately and undoubtedly contributed to his success, it also heightened the irritation he felt when he had to battle what he saw as unfair trade practices.

His inner circle in these years was small indeed. Aside from Mildred Pourciau, who began as a bookkeeper and became company treasurer and also ran the filling operation, the management team was still primarily family oriented. It consisted of his younger brother Nuppie, who would soon leave the business to start his own reconditioning plant in Birmingham, Alabama, his youngest brother Richard and his sister Leoni who had steered the company through the turbulent war years.

Aside from the ridiculous price new drums were selling for in the New Orleans market, it was becoming more and more difficult for Evans to find any steel to purchase. The United Steel Workers strike of 1959, possibly the worst strike in the steel industry's history, accentuated the shortage. These two conditions, low drum prices and unavailability of domestic steel, forced Bob into a radical decision, a decision that propelled his company to a much greater share of the new drum market and a decision that gave his competitors ammunition to undermine him in the ongoing war of words between Evans Cooperage and the big steel companies. Bob decided to buy foreign steel, particularly Japanese steel which sold for 10% - 20% less than comparable American made steel. This doesn't sound like a radical decision today, but in the late 50's and early 60's buying anything from Japan was considered a risky venture, Japanese manufacturing was considered substandard.

With Japanese steel Evans could make a profit building drums because 60% - 70% of the cost of a new drum is in the steel. Drum users were delighted, they were the ultimate winners as they were able to keep purchasing drums at depressed prices. American steel companies, however, were not about to miss the opportunity to call into question both the quality of Japanese steel as well as the depth of Bob's patriotism. After all, didn't we fight a war to beat these industrial upstarts? And just look at the imitation Zippo lighters, they were jokes. Japanese steel must be a joke too.

What they didn't mention to Bob's customers was that Japanese steel plants, built with American money and engineering know how, were among the most modern and efficient in the world. Japanese steel was not a joke, what it was, unfortunately for domestic producers, was better and cheaper than American steel and for good reason. The American Government had virtually underwritten the second modernization period of Japan's industrial infrastructure. This period of modernization which included the rebuilding of the steel industry had come during the Korean War when the American Government needed to manufacture the machinery of destruction as close to the front as possible.

The Truman and Eisenhower Administrations' obsession with preventing the spread of communism fueled a foreign policy initiative to rebuild the economies of countries hostile to communism and this led to Japan's Phoenix like rebirth. In the latter 1950's, the U.S. poured nearly 200 million dollars directly into the Japanese steel industry. In today's dollars that would be somewhere around $4 billion! Technical know how was provided through numerous trade missions between the two countries. Indeed, the U.S. Government pointed to Japan as a shining example of how successful this foreign policy strategy was, boasting with provincial audacity, "if the Japanese can make quality steel, anybody can." Of course this only made the American steel companies look foolish, as their container divisions continued barbed assaults on small time producers like Evans Cooperage, accusing them of unfair advantages because they were using cheaper foreign steel, the same foreign steel that was virtually subsidized by the U.S. government.

Jimmy Richoux was a wide eyed twenty-one year old kid, fresh from college when Bob Evans sent him to fetch the first order of steel from the Japanese ship. Richoux remembers boarding the "Vicksburg" an old riverboat converted into a steel barge and coming along side the "Maru Commander," a shiny, state of the art ocean going merchant ship. "We had thirty-seven coils of steel coming and it was down at the bottom of the hold," Richoux explains. "We had to wait for hours as they unloaded one load of consumer goods after another. Now this was the early 1960's, remember. They finally off loaded our steel and as we started back toward the Harvey terminal, I'll never forget turning around and watching them load that ship up again. Into the hold they were packing huge stacks of wooden sticks, bundles of rags, sacks of oyster shells, just the most basic raw materials. I couldn't help but wonder, how can they be sending us consumer goods when we are shipping back oyster shells. Of course I later learned that those oyster shells were used for buttons, the rags were recycled into new cloth and the sticks, I don't know, they probably used them for chop sticks. I'm not sure I realized it then, but it didn't take long for me to figure out that if the Japanese were able to trade electronic goods for oyster shells they were going to be worldwide players soon."

Soon barges loaded down with shiny coils of steel produced in the Orient began pouring into the Harvey wharf with great regularity and the Evans manufacturing division commenced a steady upward spiral of growth. Once again, a simple, decisive action had paved the way for Evans Cooperage to progress to the next level. Sales in 1962 reached almost $3 million, which was a lot of money thirty-five years ago especially for a backyard cooperage company born in the heart of the depression. But the epochal growth of Evans was yet to come.

Bob's battle with the steel industry in general and with their container divisions specifically was a constant one and he was forced to frequently and passionately defend his usage of foreign steel. Again and again, his giant corporate competitors tried to undermine Evans accounts by reminding them that, God forbid, Evans used foreign steel in their drums. This underhanded strategy would probably have had more impact in a place like Birmingham, Alabama, for despite all of its apparent southerness, New Orleans has always been a very cosmopolitan town. The port of New Orleans has seen a melting pot of people and products flood into the city for hundreds of years and the unique ethnic mix of the people has made New Orleans a most tolerant city. Most Evans customers simply didn't give a damn that they were purchasing drums made with Japanese steel. They knew that they could rely on the product and if they did have a problem, they could talk to the president of the company directly, a personal touch that the big steel drum divisions couldn't match.

The demise of the American steel industry coincides with significantly increased imports of foreign steel and industry supporters generally lay the blame for their failures on imports. While there is no denying that imported steel helped to drive the nail into the coffin of the monolithic domestic steel industry as we once knew it, the major blows were driven by a combination of misguided management that did little to prevent the aging of its vital infrastructure, rigid and increasingly out-of-touch labor unions, protective legislation and unfair trade practices that ultimately crippled an industry's ability to compete. In short, a lack of competition coupled with the general malaise of heavy industry in the United States, left a once proud and incredibly powerful industry writhing on its death bed.

(Postscript - Thankfully, the patient didn't die and today a trimmed down steel industry, albeit just a shadow of what it once was, is once again producing a quality product and beginning to grow. With the lessons of the past to both haunt and guide them, American steel companies today are more nimble than many of their foreign competitors and better positioned to move into more profitable specialty steel production.)

CHAPTER FIVE

STRIKING BACK

When Bob Evans first decided to build fifty-five gallon steel drums forty years ago, New Orleans was the drum manufacturing capitol of the world. There were three major steel companies with drum divisions and plants, the market was saturated. It took an audacious man just to consider competing against such a brood of industrial heavyweights, but as Bob says, "I didn't know if I could sell drums or not but I did know that I had to build them first before I could find out." Today, no major steel company owns or operates a drum plant in New Orleans and aside from a smaller, independent operating out of the old U.S. Steel plant, Evans is the dominant player in the market. They are the largest drum builder in the south and one of the largest in the country. They are also one of the largest reconditioners in the country. Evans didn't achieve this lofty stature in the drum industry easily. The drum plants owned by the major steel companies certainly did not go meekly into the night. They went down kicking, clawing and slinging mud.

When Bob's competitors couldn't convince Evans' customers to abandon ship because Evans used foreign steel and when the perversion of reciprocity failed to bring Evans to its knees, one steel company in particular chose a still dirtier course in trying to smear Evans' hard won reputation for quality and integrity. Lester Trilla, Bob's dear friend and associate was a wheeler and dealer to be sure but undoubtedly an honest man. However, he did little to dispel the rumor that he was somehow gangster related. Indeed, he seemed to like the intrigue the association created and more than once told Bob that he felt that it gave him an advantage when dealing with people. A Chicago native of Italian heritage, Trilla also looked the part with his dark handsome features and intense eyes.

Bob Evans knew Les Trilla for more than thirty years and when Bob Evans knows a man, he knows him rather well He is not given to casual relationships. Although they were the best of friends, if Bob had felt for one moment that Trilla was really a mobster, he would not have hesitated to sever their relationship. While there were things in Trilla's past that Bob didn't know or care about, his unwavering belief in right and wrong and profound sense of fair play would have made it impossible for him to do business with, or even associate with, a mobster. Therefore, when rumors started circulating in the early 60's, that Evans had ties to the mob, Bob went through the roof with anger. With typical passion inspired by vengeance, he relentlessly tracked down the source of the rumor. A purchasing agent of a major oil company, after swearing Bob to confidentiality, revealed that a certain executive at a certain steel company drum plant, was responsible for the rumor.

When Bob explained the situation to Les Trilla, Trilla laughed, he didn't consider it to be a big issue and advised Bob to forget about it, or better yet, to play along with it. "Let them think we're gangsters," Trilla joked, "then they will think twice about squeezing us." Bob Evans has never been good about forgetting about anything, his memory is elephant-like and he has a powerful desire to seek retribution. While he felt compelled to defend his friend, he also wanted to protect his company's hard won reputation. He agonized over what to do. If he revealed the perpetrator of the rumor and went after him for character assassination he would be forced to betray his informant. His blood boiled as he tried to think of a way to punish this person. In the end Bob reluctantly took Trilla's advise and did nothing, he had given the purchasing agent his word and his word was his bond. He had the last laugh anyway because it wasn't many years later when this major steel company decided to close down their New Orleans drum plant. Indeed, Bob couldn't help but gloat as he witnessed his eponymous company out last all the competition.

In 1959 the United Steel Workers struck all the major mills and steel production ground to a halt in the United States. This was a crippling blow for the steel industry as the bitter strike dragged on and on. The strike caused terrible shortages and delays for customers and hastened the demand for foreign steel. Ironically, the restriction of foreign steel imports was the one thing that management and labor agreed on and eventually, several "Buy American" acts, both voluntary and mandatory would be forced on U.S. manufacturers as a result of the strike. Even after the strike was settled, the steel industry was often beset by shortages and delays, the sorry truth is they never fully recovered from the '59 strike. While the big mills showed preference for their biggest customers, like the auto and appliance companies, small producers like Evans were sorely hurt by these shortages and unreliable deliveries. This was a major reason why other small manufacturers followed the lead of Evans and began to rely more and more on foreign steel. The quality was equal to if not higher than domestic steel and although the steel was being shipped halfway around the world, delivery schedules were usually more reliable.

Another major reason that Evans was able to compete and often beat the major steel companies in the drum business was and still is, because of an extremely loyal, hard working, non union work force. From the beginning, Bob Evans always looked after his hourly employees and while the work was often grueling, the pay, especially the overtime pay, made it worthwhile. Bob Evans was also clearly ahead of his time when it came to hiring minorities. When you think about the times, the late 50's and early 60's, and the place, the deep south, it was unusual to say the least when a man was hired based on his ability and not his color. While Bob Evans would never consider himself a liberal, his well paid work force was mostly black and his right hand person in the executive suite was a salty woman, and this was long before the civil rights movement gained momentum.

But these were heady days for organized labor and as Evans grew and prospered, first the Teamsters and then later the United Steel Workers sensed an opportunity. Labor abhorred a non union shop and they began to organize Evans in late 1960. Initially, Bob was absolutely determined to keep the Unions out of his plants, the thought of having someone else, even his own workers, dictate their terms to him was simply unacceptable. However, Bob eventually softened his stance, the unfortunate reality was that he would have to learn to live with labor unions, at least to some extent. He was just about to sign a contract with the Teamsters that he felt was fair to both labor and management when out of the blue, the Steel Workers, who were openly hostile to management, petitioned for and won an election. The Steel Workers were completely inflexible in their demands for a union shop and in the early summer of 1962 the situation reached an impasse, a strike seemed inevitable.

The other issues on the table included the standard pay hikes, increased vacation time and paid sick days. Bob was not wholly opposed to any of these items and a compromise probably could have been worked out without a strike. What Bob Evans strenuously objected to and what the union demanded, was a union shop. This disturbed Bob's strong belief in the ultimate power of the individual. He considered it immoral to make a man join a union just to go to work. Also he knew that if the Steel Workers won the right to a closed shop he would be saddled with their adversarial tactics forever. Bob refused to give ground on this issue all summer long and finally, in mid August, 1962, a strike was declared.

From its hostile inception to its bitter end four months later the strike was contentious and at times violent. Workers were forced to choose sides.

Approximately 60% of the work force struck and did all they could do to make life unbearable for the 40% who stayed on the job. Janice Evans remembers arriving at the plant in her car on the first day of the strike, a hot, stifling Louisiana afternoon. The orderly picket line had already degenerated into an angry mob and they stopped Janice's car at the gate. Inwardly terrified but outwardly composed, she endured their ugly jeers as they rocked her car back and forth. She felt like she was in an inferno with her windows and doors locked. "Look at her, she drives a Cadillac," the striking workers hissed. Janice was stunned by their anger. She knew many of the men personally and considered them friends, some had been to her home. Now these same men were taunting her and calling her husband horrible names. Finally, after six hours they let her pass and she made her way to Bob's office.

Inside the office it was like the ward room of a naval ship. Bob, Mildred, Richard, Leoni, and Jimmy Richoux who was at the time an hourly employee and one of the first men to cross the picket line, were mapping out their strategy. Bob was on the phone with his labor attorney from the firm of Kullman and Lang in the city. "This is going to get ugly and even uglier before it gets better," the attorney told Bob, "and the press and the police will be on their side too. Are you sure you want to stand up to that?" Bob was sure, damned sure and he asked the lawyer to file a temporary injunction forcing the strikers to let people through the picket line without risk of injury. Bob then told everyone in his office that he not only intended to fight the union but he was going to break the union and that they were in for a long, tough fight. "We may have to roll up our sleeves and work in the plant," he told his management team. "But if that's what it takes to keep this company going then that's what we will do."

The lawyers were right, the police and firemen sympathized with the strikers and were slow to react when violence erupted. Five times fires were set on Evans property as the strikers tried in vain to stop production and force Bob to negotiate. The paint booth, which was highly flammable was the usual target, but they also torched Bob's secretary's car and a company truck. But Bob was resolute, he would not even consider a closed shop and as the violence and anger escalated, his resolve strengthened.

The strike dragged on and in spite of the best efforts of everyone who crossed the picket lines, business was dropping off drastically. Even the best customers were hesitating to place orders for new drums as delays mounted. Evans needed more hands in the plant if it was going to survive.

In a daring move that openly defied the union, Bob hired a group of non union workers from Mississippi. The problem was how was he going to get them into the plant? Borrowing an idea from Homer, Bob went with the Trojan drum. On one of Evans' largest trucks, he hid his new workers inside stacked drums. The strikers let the truck through the picket line never realizing that they were being duped. Bob then had a houseboat delivered and set up living quarters aboard so that the new workers never had to cross the line and in this way he kept building, filling and reconditioning drums in spite of the strike. Still, Evans was losing money for the first time ever, a lot of money.

The most damaging aspect of strikes is that they force everyone to choose sides and invariably leave permanent scars and divisions. Former friends become enemies and the animosity persists long after the strike is over. Even the local baker, Heebe's, in downtown Gretna, sided with the workers by distributing free day old bread to the strikers. The union recruited more of the support people Evans relied on to their side, including the tug and barge crews. As orders curtailed, Bob did everything possible to control costs. They needed to return a rented barge, which was empty and costing the company money. However, the tug Captain refused to do so and Bob became enraged.

After firing the Captain on the spot, Bob recruited Valentine Emery an unsuspecting plant worker and appointed him the new first mate. Emery, who recently retired after 47 years at Evans just shakes his head when remembering what happened next. Bob ordered him to climb aboard and cast off the lines while he fired up the "Big Mule's" twin engines. "It can't be that difficult to pilot one of these things," he told himself confidently and he pushed the gear and throttle levers forward. They were off. The tug was engaged behind the two-hundred foot long steel barge. Bob managed to navigate the Harvey Canal without much trouble. Indeed, he was feeling rather cocky when he hooked to starboard and started downstream on the Mississippi River.

What Bob didn't realize is that the current is very strong in this section of the river and he needed to anticipate his turns well in advance. The river winds around a big bend called, "The Point," in Algiers just before downtown New Orleans and "Big Mule" encountered a fierce eddy that turned the tug and barge sideways to the current. The tug careened out of control. Bob threw one engine into full forward and the other into reverse trying to bring the tug and barge around but he was caught in the grip of the current and heading right for a ship bunkered alongside a crowded wharf. He shoved the rudders hard over but the "Big Mule" would not respond. He knew that he couldn't slow down because he would have even less control on the helm, so guided by instinct he pushed both throttles forward.

All he could think about was the headline that would surely be plastered across the front page of the 'TIMES PICAYUNE'. He had already been much maligned as a heartless business owner out to break the union, now New Orleans' largest newspaper would relish announcing to the world that Bob Evans had commandeered a tug and barge and caused a spectacular collision with an unsuspecting ship lying to the Governor Nichols Wharf. "Why do I have to crash into the busiest wharf in New Orleans, where every tourist in the French Quarter can witness the disaster," Bob mumbled with despair.

He blew his horn five times, the danger signal, trying to alert the crew of the ship. Miraculously, less than 100 feet from a certain collision the current suddenly eased up and the eddy evaporated as quickly as it had formed. The tug and barge lurched hard to port. This was no time to be indecisive, Bob shoved both engines into forward and held his breath as "Big Mule" and the barge slipped past the ship with just feet to spare. As Bob steered back toward the middle of the river his hands were dripping with sweat. He delivered the barge to a terminal on the Industrial Canal and made the return trip without incident. However, as he secured "Big Mule's" lines at the Evans dock he decided to stick to running his company in the future - not his tugboats.

The strike stretched into the fall. In one dramatic move Bob asked the striking workers to come into the plant. He opened a large sack and dumped out a huge stack of one dollar bills. Most of the people in the plant, including Bob Evans, had never seen such an enormous pile of money before. "This represents one year's union dues," Bob explained, "money that otherwise could end up in your pocket." By November it became obvious that Bob was going to outlast the union.

Bob Evans has enormous self discipline. As the union began calling for negotiations, Bob made a spontaneous decision to begin a fast. For a full week he ate nothing and was sustained only by drinking water and orange juice. At frequent dinner meetings with his staff and during negotiating sessions, he deliberately ate nothing. He wanted to keep his thoughts clear and also to make a point, Bob Evans can do anything if he puts his mind to it. And he did make a point, his refusal to eat during the marathon sessions threw the union negotiators completely off their stride. Before you consider this an act of unnecessary showmanship, try fasting for a day or two much less for a week. Fasting requires total commitment, especially during a time of great stress. While there is no disputing that fasting does cleanse the mind, spirit and body it requires incredible willpower. Bob's willpower was simply too much for the Steel Workers. When Evans sued the Union for damages, the Steel Workers knew they were beaten and offered to walk away if Bob dropped the lawsuit. On Christmas Eve they officially threw in the towel, the strike was over.

Operating a large manufacturing business makes you a target for labor organizers, no matter how well you pay and treat your work force. In 1968 the Communication Workers tried to organize. Again Bob beat back the union challenge but every victory was just temporary. Bob Evans recognized the adversarial nature of labor/management relations and knew that if he played hardball with the union negotiators while treating his workers fairly, he just might keep the union bosses at bay.

Surprising to many outside observers but consistent with Bob's deep understanding of his laborers, Bob hired back many of the workers who had joined the strike. He wanted to make a point that the strike was indeed behind them, many of the men had families and were in desperate financial straits, they needed work. With a functioning work force in place and with their largest customers, the oil companies booming, Evans Cooperage Inc., was poised for a dramatic growth period.

As mentioned before, Bob Evans has few outside interests, his business and his family consumed him. He is, in his own words, "addicted to his family" but there was never a distinct line between the two. Indeed, throughout the long course of his career, every business dinner included his family as standard operating procedure. And these were not infrequent outings for when your plant is located just across the river from the French Quarter, customers, vendors and sales people go out of their way to call on you. Also, every trip Bob ever undertook, whether if was for business or pleasure his family accompanied him. He just didn't like to be away from his wife and children, he was passionately devoted to them and drew strength from their presence.

As the company grew so did the children and the twins, Robbie and Ronnie, like their father and grandfather before them, loved the business from an early age. Bob put them to work in the plant during summer breaks and they often accompanied their dad to work on the weekends, and by the way, working weekends were not uncommon at Evans then and still aren't today. The boys would get so dirty in the reconditioning plant that Bob would have to load them into the trunk of his car for the short ride home. As young Jan grew, she was also schooled in the ways of the business and with typical impartialness Bob put her to work in the plant. Mildred Pourciau however put an end to that practice.

"Where is Jan?" she asked Bob one Saturday morning. "In the plant," Bob replied casually, before adding, "working, I think she's putting cap seals on drums." "What did you say," Mildred demanded, she was the only one who could talk to Bob Evans like that. "Do you want her raped, or worse? Bob, she can work with me but she won't work in the plant." And with that Mildred marched across the street to rescue Jan. Mildred was as good as her word too. In addition to her job as Treasurer, she was also responsible for the burgeoning fill operation and she taught Jan the ropes. Today, Jan oversees all the diverse filling and packaging operations at Evans. Jeffrey, Bob and Janice's last child was born with Down's Syndrome. This was the most difficult period in Bob and Janice's life. The hospital suggested that the baby be immediately placed in a special institution. Baby Jeffrey remained in the hospital for a week while Bob and Janice agonized over what to do. When they returned to the hospital and saw their beautiful son, they knew what to do, they could not part with their child, they would bring him home and make him a part of the family.

Just as the materials shipped in drums constantly changes, from asphalt and lubricating oils, to soybean oil and tallow, to fertilizers and chemicals, the family management of Evans Cooperage began to undergo changes in the late 1950's and 60's as well. Nuppie wanted to start his own reconditioning plant in Birmingham, Alabama and Bob bought out his shares. Nuppie's plant didn't survive long and Bob hired him back. Later, significant differences of opinion arose between Bob and Richard and Leoni. There was no room for compromise, they both wanted out of the company and Bob was required to buy them out. He gave them each generous payouts over time and started to fill in his staff with non family members for the first time. He also made his first moves to expand outside of the New Orleans market as well.

In a joint venture with Les Trilla and Queen City, a Cincinnati drum company, Bob purchased a reconditioning plant in St. Louis, MO. Partnerships are rarely successful and the drum business, especially the reconditioning business is an inherently local one. Needless to say the plant didn't prosper. Bob hung on longer than his partners, eventually buying them out but in the end the plant closed down. Although Bob didn't make any money in St. Louis he did learn valuable lessons that would benefit his forthcoming expansion to Houston and Cushing in the years to come.

It was also during this period when Bob went to Washington D.C. to testify before a Senate sub-committee. The steel industry lobby was trying to sneak a law through congress that would require manufacturers who used foreign steel to emboss their products indicating that it was made with foreign steel. The practical realities of such a law would have been devastating to small producers like Evans. Although two similar bills had failed to get out of the House the year before, powerful interests were behind another version of the Senate Bill, #1634, which was introduced by Senator Keogh. The committee was headed by Louisiana Senator Russell Long. He was much impressed with Bob's candor and after Bob finished explaining how impractical the pending legislation really was, the Senator remarked, "this smells to me like restraint of trade." The law never made it out of the subcommittee.

Although there were several more attempts to restrict imported steel, the federal government never actually passed a law that required independent contractors to buy domestic steel only. The steel industry however, used xenophobia, jingoism and reciprocity to persuade several large companies to require that their vendors use only domestic steel in their products. This created an immediate confrontation for Bob Evans because his largest account, Chevron, chose to enforce a 'Buy American' policy.

John Anderson, who was the purchasing agent with the Evans account at Chevron and knew Bob quite well, had the delicate job of explaining the new corporate policy. John explained that the patriotic fervor that had hit other companies had recently enveloped Chevron and they were requiring all their vendors and subcontractors to use only domestic steel in the future. Bob said simply, "John you know that is impossible for us to comply with." John, obviously uncomfortable, tried to explain how the policy was in many ways just lip service to the steel industry and that Bob essentially only had to say he was using domestic steel for his Chevron contracts. I know you well enough to know that you won't accept that, and I respect you for that, but I feel obligated to tell you that some of our other venders are playing the game."

"Well you do know me well John, because you're right, I won't accept that."

Before the meeting was over Bob asked John Anderson to try to help explain his stance to Chevron management. John replied, "I don't think I can help you Bob."

"I didn't ask if you could help me," Bob explained, "I asked if you could try to help me."

John Anderson suggested that Bob call the top management directly and gave him names and numbers. Bob navigated through the corporate hierarchy and finally reached a high level purchasing executive in San Francisco. He started by stating how he refused to deceive anyone about where the steel in his drum came from but how important it was for Evans to maintain the Chevron account. "It is impossible to tell whether a drum is made with American or Japanese steel," Bob continued, "and I could just tell you that my drums are made with American steel. But they aren't. The way I see it, if I lie, I can keep the account but if I tell the truth I can't. I need this account desperately but not desperately enough to compromise my ideals."

Although the executive could not guarantee him anything, claiming that this was a highly sensitive matter and that an exception could only be made by the Board of Directors, he did promise to present Bob's dilemma at the next meeting.

When John Anderson called a few weeks later he was incredulous. "I don't know what you said," he told Bob, "but whatever it was, you're not only still in with Chevron, you're in stronger than ever."

John Anderson, who had come to admire Bob's talent and integrity over the years, finally decided to take him up on his standing offer to join the company. While he knew full well that he was taking a major risk to leave the security of a giant oil company for the uncertainty of a small, family owned drum company, his respect for Bob's ability and the potential to be an integral part of a developing company was too alluring to pass up.

CHAPTER SIX

PORTRAIT OF A MANAGER,

PORTRAIT OF A MAN

John Anderson was hired as a Vice President in charge of Marketing. When he asked Bob what his specific duties and responsibilities would be, Bob replied, "if I knew that I wouldn't have hired you." Bob Evans managed people individually. He was certain that John Anderson, with his extensive corporate background and the corresponding lack of flexibility in job assignments, would respond positively to the challenge of defining his own position parameters. And he did. John, who still sits on the Board of Directors became Bob's new right hand man and through his corporate networking and overall marketing skills, was a major factor in the company's dynamic growth in the 70's, 80's and 90's. John, did however, have to adjust to Bob's unabashed style.

"I remember we were having lunch at Berdou's, which was Bob's favorite restaurant before they closed, trying to land a big account. Bob was in a talkative mood and insisted on telling the purchasing agent more than he needed to know about the company. I kept kicking him under the table to try to get him to stop talking. Finally, he turned to me and said, John, would you stop kicking me my leg is getting sore. I'm only telling this man the truth."

Other employees Bob Evans managed with an iron fist and a short leash. Although he was undeniably hard on his staff, he was also undeniably fair. "His door was always open, believe me, there were no secrets in the executive offices, you always knew where you stood with Mr. Evans," says Bena Saucier, Bob's long time personal secretary. While he knew mistakes were inevitable, alibis were intolerable. "You had better beat him to the phone if there was a problem," says the reconditioning plant manager, Horace Williams laughing, "because if he called you first you were in deep trouble." In the end, you were judged by your performance and managers who could accept those simple yet stark ground rules, prospered. Bob Evans was not educated in sophisticated management techniques and he was too busy to attend training and management seminars. However, his natural instincts were closely related to two managerial styles that have been well documented.

First, he was by nature a micro manager, he insisted on being informed about every facet of the business and was involved in nearly every decision. While this technique succeeds for only a few and in fact, can lead to ultimate failure, it worked for Bob Evans because although he micro managed his firm he never lost sight of the big picture. Also, he had the physical stamina and the mental wherewithal to sustain close personal contacts with every division. Successful micro management requires total commitment to the job and total commitment was the only way Bob Evans did anything. Also, micro mangers must fundamentally understand their company and on this score, it is safe to say that in a pinch, Bob Evans could (to this day at age 83!) make his way into either the reconditioning, new drum or fill plants and after a bit of fiddling, operate any given piece of machinery. He might however, have more trouble operating his secretary's computer.

Secondly, Bob had a natural "walkabout" managerial style. He truly loved to be down in the trenches. He was fascinated by manufacturing and delighted in designing new equipment or in making older gear more efficient. During Bob's prime, he spent nearly half of every day in the plant. He inspected each work station personally, alone, he wasn't just accompanying the plant manager on a ceremonial stroll. No manufacturing detail escaped his keen eye. And he wasn't there to rally the troops with cheap motivational pep talks, he was not a glad hander, pat on the back style of manager. But he certainly had a dramatic and highly effective way of making his beliefs clear. For example, when a worker tragically died while welding, the employees were certain he had been electrocuted by faulty equipment. Bob knew this was impossible and to prove the point conclusively he picked up the very same welding unit in front of the employees turned it on and touched the electrode to his bare chest repeatedly! Nothing happened and it was later revealed that the unfortunate man had suffered a heart attack. He motivated simply by expectation, an unorthodox method maybe, but an effective one just the same.

Somehow if something is expected of you, you usually find a way to do it and soon you begin to have higher expectations yourself.

"He was like Patton," says Elliot Arendt, who was an Industrial Maintenance Engineer for 30 years. "Mr. Evans never wanted anything to interrupt production, production was his God and he was down in the plant making sure that things ran smoothly. He inspired just by being there. I think most of the men were motivated by equal doses of fear and respect. I know I never met a man I admired more."

Bob Evans was not an easy man to work for. "I remember when I was hired," Arendt continues, "the man who hired me, Leonard Lively was his name, said, now Elliot think about this carefully because Mr. Evans is a hard man to work for. Well I took the job and found out that old Leonard was right. I soon learned that Mr. Evans had a graphic way of making a point. I remember him telling the plant foreman that he wanted the lights turned out in the employee lounge during working hours. Well the foreman didn't take him seriously, or maybe he just forgot about it. This went on for a week or so and then one morning, while we were all drinking our coffee just before starting time, Mr. Evans came down to the lounge. He looked the foreman straight in the eye and said calmly, 'leaving a light on is a small thing but if you can't take care of small things then how can you deal with big things.' And with that he picked up a broom and shattered the light". "Now the light is out," he said and walked out of the room.

"I quit twice during my thirty years yet in the end, I can't imagine working for a more honest and respectful man," Arendt explains with a sincere grin. "The truth is, honesty is a tough commodity to have to face every day of the week, every hour of the day but Mr. Evans demanded honesty and with honesty comes respect. Mr. Evans always told me he'd rather be respected than liked." Bob rarely if ever fired or layed off an hourly employee. He knew that they were the heart of everything. He never forgot those seven long years manning the line in the old Chickasaw Cooperage plant and he could relate to the special wants and needs of plant workers and inspire them to put forth incredible effort when the job demanded it. Over the years the Evans hourly employees have been remarkably loyal and it is not unusual to have two or even, on rare occasions, three generations at work under one roof. This is even more impressive when you consider the nature of the work, industrial drum plants can only achieve a certain degree of automation, there will always be a lot of hard physical labor involved.

Although delegating authority was not his strong suit, Bob was shrewd at getting the most out of people. John Anderson recalls how Bob called him into his office one day and told him he was about to give him the toughest job he would ever have. John racked his brain wondering what Bob had up his sleeve and Bob let the suspense build. Finally he said, "you're going to take Ronnie and Robbie under your wing and teach them everything there is to know about sales." John Anderson knew that this was not a casual assignment, when Bob rendered an order that involved his family, it was meant to be taken very seriously.

John took to his new task with enthusiasm. The two boys would work in the plant after school and then have a marketing session in John's office before trudging home to do their homework. "What amazed me about those kids," John explains with a proud smile, "is how much they wanted to learn.

They were hungry to know the business, inside and out. This was never a case of a father badgering his kids to come into the business, if anything, Bob made it as hard as possible for them. He was not given to nepotism, in fact, the troubles with his own siblings placed an even heavier burden on the boys, but they accepted the challenge."

As the boys grew, John occasionally took them on sales trips with him. He remembers taking Ronnie on a trip to Shreveport. They checked into a small motel and made their sales calls. As they were preparing to leave, John decided to bring the room copy Yellow Pages directory with them, it had all the addresses and numbers they needed. Ronnie, who was about sixteen at the time, was greatly offended and flatly insisted that they leave the Yellow Pages behind. Ronnie is much like his father and harbors the same, almost fanatical, sense of honesty.

Indeed, regarding Ronnie's honesty Bob tells a story about a family trip over the Easter holiday to the small city of Downsville near Monroe, Janice's hometown in the northeast corner of the state. It was Good Friday, the day when good and not so good Catholics are duty bound to abstain from eating meat of any kind. It seems Ronnie's aunt, who was not a Catholic, had accidentally served the children a meat sandwich for lunch while they were at her house visiting. Upon returning home, Janice asked what her sister had served for lunch and Ronnie, who was about seven at the time, blurted out, "a meat sandwich," before realizing his sin. Immediately he recanted, saying instead, "oh no, it wasn't a sandwich, it was gumbo." Janice knew Ronnie was fibbing because her sister had never made gumbo because gumbo is a dish particular to the southern part of the state. Nevertheless, Ronnie refused to admit his mistake. He was torn, he didn't want to lie but also he didn't want to cause his aunt unnecessary grief.

Bob, decided to have a little fun with his son and suggested that he and Ronnie take a walk. As they made their way into town. Bob good naturedly accused Ronnie of eating the meat sandwich and teased him that he was risking damnation. Ronnie denied the accusation but Bob could see the troubled look in his son's innocent young eyes. Ronnie continued to deny the charges as they reached a small Catholic Church. Bob directed Ronnie inside, and risking damnation of his own, acted the part of confessor. Inside the confessional he gave Ronnie one last chance to admit his error. Ronnie, deeply pained still denied any wrong doing. Right then Bob screamed out, wincing in pain he dropped to the floor and clutched his chest in mock agony.

"Ronnie," Bob croaked, "please, tell me the truth before I go."

"I did, I did eat the sandwich, I'm sorry daddy," confessed his terrified son.

Ronnie and Robbie grew up in the drum business. They started working in the plants as mere children and although the subject was rarely discussed with their father, there was little doubt that they were being groomed to one day assume the reigns of the company. "Those boys were always over here," say Bena Saucier, "either in the plant or in the office and they worked too, at least most of the time. But they were boys and they could cause a little trouble also, shooting rubber bands, whooping and hollering when their daddy wasn't around."

"We never resented the hard work," explains Robbie Evans, who worked with his father and brother until 1983, when he decided to break away and start his own company. "And yes Ronnie and I competed at everything. Dad encouraged it, I mean he gave us boxing gloves when we were four years old."

Robbie chuckled remembering his father's constant attention and instruction. "He was possessive of our time, after dinner we always sat together and had discussions. Current events, history and of course, business were the usual topics. There was always a lesson to be learned, a moral to the story. Then of course there was the time when we moved to a new house and he decided that we had been watching too much television and not reading enough. So in the new house he banished the TV to the garage! All winter long Ronnie, Jan and I froze to death if we wanted to watch a show. In fact, once that old TV died Dad refused to buy another one and we went three or four years without a TV. Dad wanted us to become readers and it worked, it was easier and a lot warmer to stay inside and read. Ronnie and I became avid readers and even plowed through the encyclopedias. If you are looking for a portrait of Dad as a manager then you have to study the portrait of the man because there isn't any difference. My father tolerated mistakes but never excuses." Robbie's point is well made, it is impossible to separate the man from the manager, Bob Evans is a passionate man and whether it was with a brand new employee in the reconditioning plant or his own child, he demanded his/her best effort all the time.

After graduating from high school, Ronnie and Robbie enrolled at Louisiana State University of New Orleans, which later became the University of New Orleans. They were reluctant students, they both were hungry to work and get on with life in what they perceived as the real world, the bustling world of Evans Cooperage. Impressively, each put in a forty hour work week at Evans while attending University full time. Nothing less was expected of them and while they graduated with business degrees on schedule they were also schooled, albeit in a hands on way, in every aspect of the drum business. In addition to John Anderson, their mentors included John Smith, Henry Legendre and Uncle Lester Trilla.

Young Janice, who as it turns out is much like her father, dreamed of becoming a doctor. Although she also worked at Evans during the summers and weekends, she wasn't enthralled with the business as a child, it wasn't pulsing through her veins the way it was with her brothers. Her father, who saw a natural business acumen in his daughter, tried to convince her to study business when it was time to go off to University. Jan was interested in science and determined to be a doctor until a counselor at Louisiana State University in Baton Rouge convinced her to shift her major to nursing by warning her that she would never be able to have a family if she became a doctor. This was still the pervading belief in the south twenty years ago, doctoring was a man's job and a woman should be content to be a nurse, if indeed, she insisted on working at all.

A stint of summer hospital work hinted to Jan that nursing might not be her calling after all, a notion that had been brewing in her mind ever since her dreams of becoming a doctor had been shot down. Life can be so complicated when you're twenty years old, a simmering romance was also muddling her plans. She had met Gary Hamilton as a freshman in Baton Rouge on a blind date. Gary insists that she accepted the date only because he had highly sought after tickets to an Elton John concert. Although he was immediately smitten with her, she was determined not to get serious with any boy so soon.

But love is urgent when you are young, Jan and Gary were soon dating and in spite of themselves, getting very serious.   But the lurking specter of Bob Evans was never far away.

Jan's condition for going away to school was that she had to maintain a 3.0 grade point average. After her freshman year she fell just short but in the Evans household a rule was a rule, Jan was not allowed to return to Baton Rouge. Jan's mom tried to intervene on her behalf, Janice often felt that Bob was too tough on the kids, but Bob's rules were cast in cement. And besides, Jan was really the apple of his eye and Bob admits that he liked the idea of having her closer to home. Instead of returning to LSU she attended a local nursing college for the next couple of years.

Gary, who was older, soon graduated with a degree in Agricultural Education. However, the required student teaching convinced him that he didn't enjoy teaching and soon he was back in school, working toward a master's degree in Agricultural Economics. Their relationship survived the distance between Gretna and Baton Rouge and Gary was a frequent weekend house guest.

"Mr. Evans intimidated me right from the start," Gary says with a laugh. A one time interim President and today a company Director, not to mention Vice President, Controller and Treasurer, Gary Hamilton was a shy farm boy when he met Mr. Evans for the first time. "Sitting down for the traditional Evans family Sunday dinner was quite daunting," Gary explained, "and I quickly realized that if you couldn't talk business, specifically the drum business, you didn't do much talking. They weren't especially interested in learning how to milk cows."

Soon Jan and Gary were engaged and one can sympathize with Gary while picturing him formally asking for Jan's hand. By this time Gary had become close friends with Robbie and Ronnie and now that he was soon to be part of the family, they thought that he should consider working for Evans. Bob liked the idea too but there was one condition. He insisted that Gary obtain a graduate degree in business administration. "If you are going to have a future with us," he told Gary in his typically direct manner, "then you'll need that degree and you might as well get it now."

So Gary, who felt like he was destined to be a perpetual student, enrolled at the University of New Orleans and set about finishing the sixty-six hours he needed for his MBA. He also moved into a small, one room apartment above the plant that Bob had graciously made available. "You'll be close to work and you can save some money," Bob told him in all seriousness. In addition to his graduate work, Gary was also a so called "management trainee" with an hourly wage of $4.50. "Management trainee was the family word for laborer," Gary says today, adding, "I worked in the new drum plant, learning the business, as Mr. Evans told me, in the best way possible, from the ground floor up. Oh what a man will do for love."

The new guard, Ronnie, Robbie and Gary were soon to be joined by Jan. Shortly after she and Gary were married, she concluded that nursing was not her life's calling. "Besides," she says laughing, "I wanted to make more money." She approached her father about the possibility of working at Evans. "I'd like to hire you," Bob told his daughter, "but the problem is, I don't need a nurse." Jan steamed. "Well daddy, you know I can do things other than nursing." "If you learn to type you can work as a secretary, Bob said to his daughter sarcastically." "Daddy," Jan was becoming exasperated, "what do I have to do make more money?" Bob Evans knew he had his daughter right where he wanted her for he never doubted that she had natural business talent and would prove to be a great asset to the company. "You'll need some business training," he told her. "If you go back to school and get a business degree then we can probably find some work that will challenge you." Today Jan Hamilton is a Director and Secretary/Treasurer of Evans Industries and manager of packaging services.

The drum business is by nature a relatively local one, new drum manufacturing, reconditioning and filling operations need to be close to shipping points and there must be a thorough understanding of your customer's needs and constant communication. Also, concerning reconditioning, there is a practical limit to how far you can range in collecting used drums. Recognizing this, Bob knew that if Evans was to successfully expand much beyond the New Orleans market he had to build or buy plants in new markets. Over the years he had a few joint ventures with Trilla, Queen City Barrel and other drum companies but joint ventures and partnerships are rarely successful. Therefore in 1980, when he decided the time was right to build a new drum plant near Houston he never considered taking in a partner. At this stage of his business career Bob Evans was rather confident of his own abilities and rightly so. Also, he had the internal resources for much of the capitalization and could limit his long term debt. He simply didn't need or want partners.

Evans, which had outgrown the New Orleans market was looking for an avenue for expansion and a corporate decision by Texaco provided just such an avenue. Texaco, a huge user of reconditioned drums, had historically reconditioned their own drums at a large plant in Port Arthur, Texas. However, in 1978, Texaco management reeling from labor and profitability problems, decided to abandon the reconditioning business. Texaco felt it could subcontract the work and probably save money. Also they were ready to eliminate the aggravation of running a reconditioning plant. Evans was awarded a five year contract to supply Texaco with up to 400,000 drums annually and immediately began construction of a state of the art reconditioning and fill plant outside of Houston.

Although new drum manufacturing was not part of the original Houston business plan because new drum margins were still strong and warranted transporting from Harvey, in the back of his mind Bob Evans foresaw the day when he would build drums in Houston as well. The Houston facility made good sense even without the Texaco contract. The oil business was in a strong up cycle and this plant gave them a foothold in the largest oil market in the country. With Evans' unique ability to provide packaging as well as drums, they were certain to be a major player. "Bob Evans has always had the ability to look into a crystal ball and see the future of the drum business," claims John Anderson. "His instincts are incredible."

Patience however, is not one of his virtues. "Now, Now, Now," was Mr. Evans motto," says Gary Roerig, today the Harvey Plant General Manager and the person who was largely responsible for building the Houston plant. "Mr. Evans hates to waste time," Roerig explains, "we built that plant in record time." Roerig tells a story about Bob's lack of patience. "We had flown from New Orleans to Ft. Smith, Arkansas where they were auctioning off some equipment we thought we might be able to use in Houston. The auction finished early so Bob decided we should go to Houston for the rest of the afternoon. There were no flights from that tiny airport until later that night but Bob demanded that they find us a plane. He was so damned insistent that they finally rounded up a plane. And what a plane it was. We ended up on a little six seater job and had the flight of our lives, it was terrifying."

Evans continued expanding a couple years later, building a new drum assembly plant in Tulsa, Oklahoma. By producing drum parts in Harvey and then shipping them to a satellite assembly plant, Evans was able to expand quickly again but without another huge capital expense. The Tulsa plant, which was later moved to Cushing, was strategically located to provide maximum margins on sales to their expanding oil business client base in the area between Tulsa and Oklahoma City.

Even Bob Evans' crystal ball sometimes became a little cloudy. However, the sign of a successful manager is his ability not only to predict the future environment for his or her business, but also, the ability to react to sudden changes within that environment. In 1984, Texaco decided to decentralize the subcontracting of reconditioned drums to contract packagers nearer to the point of distribution. This decision scattered business to drum companies all over the country and drastically reduced business for Evans' new plant. Also, new drum prices and margins began to decline in this same period, particularly in the southwest. This was the kind of crisis that would make most managers timid.

Timid is a word that has never been used to describe Bob Evans. Instead of cowering, he gazed into his crystal ball and chose a bold course of action. He would marshal his resources and invest in the future. With tighter margins on new drums, it didn't make sense to transport them from Harvey to Houston so first, he decided to install a new drum fabrication and fill plant in the Houston facility. Secondly, oil companies were beginning to use more light gauge new drums and fewer reconditioned drums and Evans had to be prepared for this change. Bob made the biggest decision in the history of Evans Cooperage when he began construction of a brand new manufacturing plant in Harvey that would become one of the finest drum plants in the world, capable of high speed production of the highest quality lined and unlined drums. Thirdly, the process of reconditioning drums was changing. Easy to clean oil drums were giving way to difficult to clean chemical drums. The reconditioning business was being utilized more and more by paint, resin and solvent manufacturers and these drums, which often required special linings, also required specialized equipment for reconditioning. Bob invested in more efficient and environmentally friendly reconditioning technology. And finally, Bob renewed his commitment to packaging by expanding all of Evans' filling facilities.

While these projects proved extremely costly, nearly $28 million in expenditures above operating and maintenance costs, amazingly, Evans managed to internally fund most of it and came away with just $6 million in long term debt. There is no doubt that the strong financial base and broad market share that the company enjoys today is a dividend of those bold investments of a decade ago. Bold decisions come naturally for Bob Evans. Take the story of the high speed helium leak tester for example.

"One of the reasons I admire Bob Evans so much is the trust he has had in me over the years," says Jimmy Richoux, Vice President of Purchasing and also actively involved in new technology development. "And believe me, the helium tester not only tested drums but the process of building it tested Mr. Evans' as well. You see, he is not the most patient man in the world."

Helium leak testing, which utilizes a mass spectrometer to detect the presence of helium, provides the most accurate method of leak detection available for 55 gallon steel drums, rendering more common leak test methods obsolete. At the time the new Evans manufacturing plant in Harvey was completed, there were a couple of different helium leak testers operating in European drum plants but these were custom installations. To order an engineering firm to design and install a helium leak tester would have been prohibitive. There was another problem as well, the Evans line speed was too fast for existing helium tester technology. Bob Evans' solution to the problem typifies his approach to business. "We'll build our own," he announced to an incredulous Jimmy Richoux, "and it will not only handle our line speed, it will also be more accurate than any existing tester."

Richoux, who is a self taught design engineer, was stunned. "A helium leak tester is a fairly complex piece of equipment," he says with classic understatement. Undaunted, he and Bob spent months, working into the wee hours night after night, designing their own helium leak detector. "We purchased a mass spectrometer and made it work for our line." When it was finally built and installed, to Jimmy's relief (Bob never doubted it) it could handle Evans peak, 800 drums per hour while detecting leaks so minute that most liquids wouldn't pass through them. "Mind you, we had some problems," Richoux says smiling, "but we kept improving it until we were satisfied." And it is accurate. "If there is a problem it's that we reject drums that other companies sell because it is so precise." Richoux is justly proud of the tester and notes, "it's been running flawlessly for years and we have even built and sold two testers to other drum companies."

The monolithic closure system is a technological break through that only Bob Evans had the vision to fund. Jointly developed by Ty Techera, Jimmy Richoux and Bob Schurr, this unique system forms a flange directly out of the parent metal of the drum head, thereby reducing costs by eliminating flange gaskets and flange gasket failures, which sometimes cause drum leakage. With the monolithic system, the flange cannot be dislodged from the drum because it is an integral part of the drum head. "This design concept sounds deceptively simple," says Techera, a special consultant for Evans Industries, "but the manufacturing processes for making a practical application are quite complex. Bob Evans knew this going in and he encouraged us to stay with it. He realized that this might be the single most important improvement to the steel drum since its inception and he insists that Evans be involved in its development."

The business side of Bob Evans is hard edged, both brilliant and brutal, imaginative and relentless, fair but unyielding. But there is a softer side, a side he tries to keep hidden, a side that not everyone sees. Bob Evans is a generous man, a devoted family man and through the long, circuitous course of a lifetime Bob Evans has quietly revealed his soft side again and again.

Brief snapshots from diverse perspectives leave lasting impressions of a different Bob Evans.

"The Bob Evans that most people don't know," says Diane Richoux, Jimmy's charming and diminutive wife, "is the man who always brought his family along on business dinners. I mean the whole family, Janice, the twins, Jan and Jeffrey. Jeffrey is handicapped and a real sweetheart, there was never any question that he would be included in family activities." Ernest Pitts, a driver who worked for Evans for 34 years recalls how Mr. Evans made a truck available to help his sister move when she was down and out. Beverly Anderson, John's wife, recalls how she received an unexpected check in the mail before a trip to Europe. Pablo Maique says, "Mr. Evans gave me a chance when nobody else would." Sharad Saraf, the manager of a Bombay company manufacturing drum parts that Bob helped gain a foot hold in the U.S. market says, "Bob Evans is my guru." Jay Horman, Vice President of Marketing and Sales, says, "Bob Evans' philosophy of not only meeting but exceeding customer expectations is still the order of the day at Evans."

It is his family that truly knows the soft side of Bob Evans best exemplified by the enduring love his children have for him. And while he has always been demanding his love for them has also been unbounded. Then, of course, there is the unfaltering relationship of Bob Evans and his lovely bride of 43 years, Janice. While Bob is the force that drives the family forward, Janice is the glue that holds it all together. Family and friends often joke that Janice should be sainted for putting up with Bob's devotion to his business but she knows love is a two way street and Bob has always been steadfastly devoted to her. Perhaps Gary Hamilton, who has had the unique vantage of

seeing all the different sides of his father in law sums it up best. "Bob Evans'
legacy in both life and business, will be his family."

CHAPTER SEVEN

AT HOME

The days are quieter for Bob Evans now that he is semi-retired at age eighty-four. He doesn't make it into the office every day although his sage council is just a phone call away and as Chairman of the Board he is still instrumental in all major decisions. Most of the discussions that were eventually shaped into this book took place, over the course of a year, in the solarium of Bob's home. Together with Janice, we gathered in this sun drenched room, resplendent with plants and flowers and gradually recalled and reconstructed the events, decisions, reactions and anecdotes that comprised the sum of one man's amazing life. Sipping coffee, often laughing and always scribbling furiously, I was aware that I would never be able to capture all the material that should go into this book, although I am hopeful that I have managed to present the essence of the man. The more time I spent with Bob Evans the more I realized how privileged I was to be able to share these many hours with this proud, accomplished, inspiring man. Naturally I interviewed many people while conducting research for this book, from past and present employees to customers to industry peers. In the end however, it is the persona of Bob Evans, sitting quietly in the morning sun, remembering the early days and contemplating what the future may hold that gives this book life. For it is his story and it is his book.

Bob and Janice live in a lovely home in Gretna, not far from where Bob grew up and only minutes from the plant. Bob not only designed the house, he also acted as the subcontractor, overseeing every phase of its construction. The result is magnificent, a stately brick colonial dominated by wide, open, airy rooms. The floors are teak parquet, like in a fine yacht, the ceilings are trimmed in simple yet elegant facades and the fireplace is French marble. The Evans' have decorated the house with style, combining the flavor of New Orleans with accents from their worldwide travels. The grounds are extensive, well manicured and line the fifth hole of the country club golf course. However, the feature that Bob likes best about the house is that it is right next to Jan and Gary's house and Ronnie's house is just around the block. The grandchildren are never far way, their voices fill the house with joy.

Indeed, as I met with Bob and Janice to talk about this final chapter, they were making preparations for a three week trip to Turkey, Greece and France. They were to be accompanied by their daughter Jan and three of their grandchildren. It seems clear that the Evans tradition of including the children in almost every activity will endure into the next generation.

This first of two topics that I have come to discuss with Bob this morning is not an easy one to talk about, in fact, it is still a bit painful for Bob to plow through the details again. There won't be as much laughter today, Bob's scars only recently healed. There will be however, reflection, understanding, optimism and not surprisingly, wisdom. I have come to talk about the transition that took place a couple of years ago when Bob was asked to step down as company President and Ronnie assumed the reins of day to day operations.

The transfer of power is probably the single most difficult task a successful entrepreneur must contend with. Lets face it, it is extremely tough for the person who built a company from the ground floor up, who took all the risks along the way, who alone made the bold decisions that allowed the company to prosper, to suddenly realize that the curtain is falling and that it is time for the next act to begin. As your company, a company that bears both your name and your imprint, sails toward the distant horizon you are no longer the captain or the navigator. Most entrepreneurs find it impossible to believe that the company can exist without them. When this proverbial passing of the torch involves a father and son the transition is even more formidable and the odds of success are remote. As all fathers know, we alone know what is best for our children and they should never question our judgment.

There are many well documented cases of entrepreneurs refusing to yield power and literally having to be forced out of their own companies. In the case of Evans Industries, the new guard, the young Turks, Ronnie, Jan and Gary had to use their combined clout as stockholders and board members to convince their father/father-in-law to step down. It was not pleasant for anyone involved and at times became extremely trying even nasty, yet in the end, reason and understanding prevailed as the family did the right thing.

The transition period actually began when Ronnie decided to leave the company in 1990 after working side by side his father for many years. "We both felt so strongly about the company that we were often in conflict," Ronnie explains, adding with a wry grin, "and dad usually wins most conflicts." Ronnie started his own firm, importing drum parts and brokering industrial blow molding equipment. "Looking back, that year out of the company was the best thing that I could have done," Ronnie says, "I needed some breathing room."

Bob, however, was steering the company through shoal waters, the early 90's were tough times in the drum business. Bob missed both Ronnie's talents and the camaraderie that only a son can provide. In many ways he felt abandoned and whenever he and Ronnie were together Bob passionately urged Ronnie to reconsider his decision and return to the company. He was relentless and anyone who knows Bob Evans knows that his version of relentlessness is unique. He had lost Robbie when he left the company and started a business of his own and he didn't want to lose Ronnie the same way.

After much soul searching Ronnie finally agreed to come back to the company. Ronnie has always had a flair for sales and customer relations and he agreed to be the acting National Sales Manager for an interim period, to help the company through the tough times it was experiencing and then, once the company was on firm financial ground, he would honestly evaluate whether or not he could continue to work with his father in the future. Ronnie insisted that Bob yield more authority and to act more in accordance with the desires of the Board of Directors. But that is not Bob Evans' style. Bob Evans has never shirked or skirted responsibility, he has always been willing to make the tough calls and rightly or wrongly he stands fast by his decisions. Conversely, he has never liked sharing responsibility with anyone and instinctively dislikes management by committee. Also, Bob had managed, despite severe physical ailments, to guide the company back toward profitability and with Ronnie back in the fold, was feeling heady about the drum business and the long term prospects for Evans. But Ronnie was resolute, Bob had to release the strangle hold he had on all company decisions. A showdown became inevitable. Either Ronnie left the company for good or he challenged his father for the leadership of Evans Industries. A showdown came. When the dust settled, the new guard had carried the day.

"Ronnie is more like me than I realized," Bob says with a sardonic smile, "I understand that he did what he had to do and I respect him for that. It was tough on both of us, to say the least." There is no denying that for a while Bob was bitter and the kids were wracked with guilt. However, plenty of hard work and bridge building, particularly by Ronnie's wife Patsy who at times single-handedly kept the family lines of communication open, rekindled the deep love and respect that has kept the Evans clan so close for so long. Today, Bob has accepted his role as advisor to the company. Always immensely creative, now that he is free of the distractions of day to day operations he has helped position the company for the future.

"My father knows this business better than any man alive," says Ronnie, "and through his foresight, Evans is poised for continued growth." Typically, Gary Hamilton puts the matter into clear focus. "Only a family as strong as the Evans' could endure a shakeup like this and end up closer than ever before. And like usual, it was Bob Evans who led the way."

The second topic of discussion on this summer morning lights a fire under Bob and his steady eyes burn bright. We are going to discuss the future of the drum business and the role Evans Industries Inc., should play. I prepare a fresh sheet of paper and direct my first question. Bob is clearly back in his element, looking to the future with hope and vision instead of lamenting the past.

JK - Will the 55 gallon steel drum continue to be the container of choice for industry throughout the world?

RE - Yes, I believe it will. There is no doubt that packaging alternatives, like totes and plastic pails, will gradually command a larger piece of the business but the steel drum will endure. When you think about it, barrels have been around a long long time. Why? Because of their shape, they are easy to move, one man can roll a drum and the cylindrical shape is also incredibly strong. Steel drums changed the course of industry, especially the oil industry. Steel is a good material for drum manufacture because it is easy to work with and highly resistant to the dangerous chemicals that are stored and shipped in drums these days. Also, Evans is developing technology that will keep the drum at the forefront of packaging, the monolithic closure system is an example. I have no doubt that fifty years from now we will still be building and reconditioning steel drums.

JK - Do you agree with economists when they say companies must think globally if they are going to survive in the future?

RE - In some industries I believe that is true, in the drum industry however, I am not so sure. Our business is basically a local one, there is a limit to how far you can travel to find reconditioned drums and new drums must be manufactured close to the point of shipping. So, while I agree that the world's economy is becoming more integrated, I think successful drum companies should still focus on their local market. Evans has been international for many years, both in purchasing steel and fittings and by supplying technology and drums for assembly plants. There is certainly growth potential overseas but it is vital to keep your primary markets well serviced."

JK - What do you think about the state of American industry these days, particularly the state of the American steel industry?

RE - I have no doubt that the American steel industry can become healthy again. It is unlikely that they will ever dominate the world market like they did once but with that said, there is no reason we cannot manufacture steel in this country. Steel companies were among the first companies to downsize and not surprisingly they have discovered that they can build quality steel with fewer man hours. As far as American heavy industry is concerned, I think if we keep the government from interfering with business, America still has the capability to lead the world in industrial production. Our products are still highly respected and considered top quality. It is vital that we never lose that reputation. I don't believe that industrial America's best days are behind her.

JK - Do you foresee a time when drum plants will be completely automated, thereby reducing the man hours required in building and reconditioning drums.

RE - No, I don't, at least not to the extent that it is possible with other industries. The nature of drum manufacturing and reconditioning requires a certain degree of physical labor that will be very difficult to automate. I do believe that controlling labor costs is critical to successfully running a drum plant and will be even more so in the future. You should hire only the best people and expect to employ them for a long time.

JK - When you look at the state of Evans Industries Inc., today, are you pleased?

RE - Yes, absolutely. The company is well positioned with its new drum manufacturing, reconditioning and filling and packaging operations. We have the ability to be our own customer and to shift our focus quickly if the customer demands it. We have a degree of flexibility that no other drum company can match and I think that is critical to our success. With that said however, the company can never afford to rest on its laurels, never, that is a recipe for disaster. I never felt the company would be spectacular under my management and I never felt secure. I did however, feel that we had and still do have, unlimited potential to grow if we manage things properly."

JK - You took many bold risks along the way, building a backyard cooperage into a major industrial company, what risks do you see the company taking in the future?

RE - I don't think that the company will have to take as many risks as I did, at a certain level, once the business is well established, the need for major risk taking is reduced. However, it is critical to continually improve the quality of your product, and if that involves risk, then that is a risk you must take. When you stop taking risks you die, that is a simple rule of business.

JK - What steps must Ronnie take to continue to grow the business in the future?

RE - To some extent, just to continue doing what he is doing, his record to date has been excellent. I have always firmly believed that the key to success is to reinvest in the company. Acquisitions are tempting and occasionally lucrative but the long term growth of any solid company will come from pouring money back into the company. If there is one thing I have always believed in it is to reinvest in the company.

JK - When you give Ronnie advice what do you tell him, and does he listen?

RE - (Laughing) Well he seems to be listening anyway. First, I tell him what I just told you and I'll say it again, continually put your money back into the company to improve the quality of your product and to increase your market share. Secondly, I urge him to enjoy it, to savor the moment of it all because it goes by so quickly. Enjoying what you do is fundamental to doing it well. Finally, and there is no need to tell Ronnie this but I will say it anyway, always conduct your affairs with integrity.

JK - That sounds like good advice to me. I have one last question. If you were twenty-one years old again and chomping at the bit to take the world of business by storm, what business would you pursue today?

RE - There is no doubt that I would go into the drum business. I guess like my father before me, I am and always will be a cooper.

BY RONALD J. EVANS

The story of my father's life in some ways is not unlike that of other successful American businessmen who were born to humble circumstances. Words used to describe the personality traits of much more famous self made men like Henry Ford, John D. Rockefeller and J. Paul Getty apply to the guy we affectionately and respectfully call "the Old Man." Words like imagination, determination, drive, innovation and hard work.

As important as these qualities are in achieving business success, qualities dad possessed in full measure, one would not have a complete picture of my father without knowing about the values he held dear that I believe were most important in shaping his life. Values such as a great sense of honor, fidelity to one's wife, and never failing to be appreciative of someone who did you a favor. And most importantly, integrity, that is the knowledge that one could completely rely on your word, that a deal was a deal regardless of the consequences, that you would never under any circumstances tell a lie. These beliefs were not only the foundation upon which dad conducted his affairs but are additionally what he taught his children and expected from his employees.

This tough, uncompromising businessman was also a very demanding spouse and father. He, however, greatly loved and was completely dedicated to his wife and family, having few or no outside interests or friends except those made through business relationships.

The passion and love he had for his family and business was all consuming, leaving virtually no room in his life for anything else. He seldom traveled because he did not want to be away from his family, but when he did, he always tried to do so with mom and the kids. Some have theorized that this addiction to family and business was fulfilling his need to dominate and control the things in his life. There is probably a small element of truth in that. It is certain that he had great difficulty separating family issues from business issues, which at times strained the family relationship. Additionally, there have been great upheavals in the family relationships, particularly involving my brother and more recently during the transition of business authority from dad to me. But the love has endured, family relationships are stronger than ever, and dad and mom are today enjoying a most well deserved life of retirement.

Although much has changed about the way Evans Industries, Inc. does business today as compared to when dad was the at the helm, the qualities and values that epitomized dad's life continue to guide the company he built. The legacy is coupled with a new focus on customer satisfaction and a team spirit that is motivating company employees to strive for excellence and success as never before. There is no doubt that the life's work of this great man will continue to be an inspiration to the thousands of people that had the privilege of knowing him.

THE EPISODES

These episodes were written by Robert Evans over the course of a year from the fall of 1977 to the fall of 1978. They were sent to all Evans' important customers at the time including Chevron, Shell, Exxon and others. They represent Bob Evans at his caustic best and are a passionate defense of why Evans used foreign steel for manufacturing drums. They are a brutal and honest assessment of several steel company drum divisions and turned out to be a prophetic prediction of the overall demise of the American steel industry. They are reprinted here in their original format, including the cover letter that accompanies each episode.

A DIFFERENT DRUMMER

Evans Cooperage Co., Inc.

Post Office Drawer 68

MANUFACTURERS AND RECONDITIONERS
OF STEEL SHIPPING CONTAINERS

INLAND WATER TERMINAL
AND DRUMMING PLANT

Harvey, Louisiana 70059

Telephone: 366-8571

October 21, 1977

Attached is the first episode of Why Evans Cooperage Uses Foreign Steel. The number of episodes will probably total ten or more, and at this moment, six have already been produced.

They will be forwarded to you in intervals of three or four days, hoping that this will prevent you from becoming bored. We realize that some of our customers may feel that we exaggerate; however, we assure you that whereas we feel very strongly about what has happened in the past, we have tried to be fair and accurate.

I, like most business men, resent and complain about the intrusion of Washington in my business affairs. It is an unfortunate fact that Washington usually intrudes in an effort to correct an abuse. Sometimes the cure is worse than the disease; however, that does not excuse the perpetrator of the abuse.

If you carefully read all episodes of Why Evans Cooperage Uses Foreign Steel, I believe you will understand why I make this statement.

Very truly yours,

EVANS COOPERAGE CO., INC.

Robert G. Evans, President

RGE/bs

Attachment

EVANS COOPERAGE CO., INC.

POST OFFICE DRAWER 68

MANUFACTURERS AND RECONDITIONERS
OF STEEL SHIPPING CONTAINERS

HARVEY, LOUISIANA 70059

INLAND WATER TERMINAL
AND DRUMMING PLANT

October 21, 1977

TELEPHONE: 366-8571

WHY EVANS COOPERAGE USES FOREIGN STEEL

EPISODE #1

TITLE

LETS KEEP EVANS OUT OF THE DRUM MANUFACTURING BUSINESS

or

IF HE CAN'T BUY STEEL, HE CAN'T MAKE DRUMS

In 1954 Evans Cooperage, which was operating a drum reconditioning and drum filling plant, decided to start manufacturing steel drums. Located in the New Orleans metropolitan area were four producers of steel drums: Rheem Manufacturing Company, Jones & Laughlin Steel Corporation - Container Division, Inland Steel Container Company, and United States Steel Products Division.

Accordingly, Evans contacted the following steel manufacturers in an effort to purchase steel to produce drums:

1.) United States Steel Corporation
2.) Republic Steel Corporation
3.) Inland Steel Company
4.) Jones & Laughlin Steel Corporation

The above producers were contacted for the following reasons: United States Steel Corporation and Republic Steel Corporation had mills in the Birmingham, Alabama area, which was the closest steel producing area to New Orleans. Steel from these plants could be trucked to our plant in the small quantities we could afford at relatively low cost. Inland Steel Company and Jones & Laughlin Steel Corporation had drum manufacturing plants in the New Orleans area, and as a result moved steel economically in barge load quantities from Chicago and Pittsburgh. Obviously, our sharing barge loads would enable us to purchase steel cheaper in the smaller than barge load quantity that we could afford.

Since over half the cost of a steel drum is represented by the cost of steel it contains, it was most important that we purchase steel at the lowest possible delivered price.

We realized that all of the above producers of steel also produced steel drums; however, we were naive enough to believe that these firms would not refuse to sell us steel.

The realization of our innocence came about after weeks of total failure to purchase or get a commitment for even one pound of steel from any of the producers mentioned above.

This refusal to sell us steel absolutely was <u>not</u> a result of a temporary steel shortage such

-1-
continued

October 21, 1977

...s one that might result from a steel strike or the threat of a strike. We contacted these firms in advance of our immediate requirement and were seeking a long term supplier.

...t is hard to believe that all four mills contacted would have refused to sell us steel were there no connection between the fact that they produced steel drums and we were attempting to start manufacturing steel drums.

...ven if this refusal was a 1000 - 1 case of sheer coincidence, the incident indicates the necessity of foreign competition.

...ear in mind that this was 1954, fully 9 years after World War II ended, but before foreign competition was a factor.

...hereas steel was available to us from other mills in the midwest at favorable delivery prices via barge, we could not afford to purchase a full barge load at a time. Finally after considerable effort, we located a consumer of sheet steel in New Orleans who was willing to share a pool barge of steel with us which was purchased from a midwest mill that did not produce steel drums.

...aving cleared the first hurdle in securing steel and the second in building a small drum manufacturing plant, we began to produce limited quantities of drums to be used in our drum filling operation.

...ll seemed well until we were given the unexpected opportunity to sell large quantities of new steel drums in competition with the other four New Orleans area drum manufacturing plants.

...ore about this in:
        WHY EVANS COOPERAGE USES FOREIGN STEEL
        EPISODE #2 - TITLE: LETS KNOCK EVANS OUT OF THE BOX
                        or
                WE'LL CUT PRICES NOW AND RAISE THEM WHEN HE'S BROKE

EVANS COOPERAGE CO., INC.

POST OFFICE DRAWER 68

MANUFACTURERS AND RECONDITIONERS
OF STEEL SHIPPING CONTAINERS

HARVEY, LOUISIANA 70059

INLAND WATER TERMINAL
AND DRUMMING PLANT

TELEPHONE: 366-8571

October 25, 1977

Attached is Episode #2 of Why Evans Cooperage Uses Foreign Steel.

As you will note, approximately 20 years ago, The Giant started its campaign of selective price cutting aimed at Evans. This resulted in severely depressed prices of new drums that spread to other parts of the country and did finally result in the early 1970's in J & L closing its drum manufacturing plant in New Orleans due to sustained losses.

About that same time, presidents of three of the drum manufacturing subsidiaries of large steel companies, including The Giant's, were relieved of their jobs.

Whereas Evans' president kept his job, being responsible for the survival of a drum manufacturing plant under these conditions was not a pleasant experience to say the least.

Very truly yours,

EVANS COOPERAGE CO., INC.

Robert G. Evans, President

RGE/bs

Attachment

EVANS COOPERAGE CO., INC.

POST OFFICE DRAWER 68

MANUFACTURERS AND RECONDITIONERS
OF STEEL SHIPPING CONTAINERS

HARVEY, LOUISIANA 70059

INLAND WATER TERMINAL
AND DRUMMING PLANT

October 25, 1977

TELEPHONE: 366-8571

WHY EVANS COOPERAGE USES FOREIGN STEEL

EPISODE #2

TITLE

LETS KNOCK EVANS OUT OF THE BOX

or

WE'LL CUT PRICES NOW AND RAISE THEM WHEN HE'S BROKE

Evans was now producing a very limited amount of steel drums, all of which were used in its drum filling operation. None were being sold directly in competition with the other four local drum producers.

One day in the latter part of 1957, a visitor arrived unannounced stating that he was the manager of the ____ Terminal in Houston, which was filling large quantities of vegetable oil in drums for export. He stated that ____ was moving its vegetable oil filling operation from Houston to a local terminal near our plant that it had just purchased. The reason for the visit was to explore the possibility of purchasing large quantities of new drums from Evans.

Believing that the ____ representative wanted to purchase drums at deviated prices, the writer replied that he was not interested in breaking the market structure in New Orleans. The ____ representative replied that he was not expecting price concessions since he had purchased approximately 350,000 drums the previous year at list price in Houston and expected to purchase a like amount in New Orleans at list price.

The reason given for purchasing from Evans was that ____ would fill the drums on a barge in front of their terminal, and since Evans was the only drum manufacturer in the New Orleans area located on the water and additionally had barges that could be used for delivering the empty drums to ____ and the filled drums shipside from ____ Evans was a natural.

Evans agreed to sell ____ 18 gauge drums at the prevailing price of $6.87 each delivered. For many years market conditions relating to steel drums at New Orleans had been very stable with no record of price cutting. This was as true in accounts where reciprocity was a factor, as well as accounts where reciprocity was not a factor.

At the time Evans did not realize it but a new era was to begin after the agreement with ____. Before Evans had delivered its first drum to ____, one of the New Orleans drum manufacturing plants owned by a steel producer made the first move by cutting the Evans price by 27¢ per drum. Evans met the price; however, that reduced price was short lived since only months later another drum manufacturer owned by a still larger steel manufacturer cut the reduced price even more.

continued

October 25, 1977

For ease of description we will later refer to this firm as "The Giant". We consider the
Giant an arrogant law breaker that finally agreed under Department of Justice pressure to
curtail its use of reciprocity - a promise that we feel was never completely kept.

Whereas Evans' other local competitors did eventually accept Evans as a legitimate competitor
and decided to live and let live, The Giant never did and we are confident is still trying
to put Evans out of business.

The Giant continued to cut prices in the vegetable oil area in an effort to force Evans out
of business. Over a period of ten years during which time both The Giant and Evans experienced 9 steel increases and 10 labor increases, The Giant continued to cut prices.

Finally after 10 years of price cutting, that $6.87 drum was selling at $5.75. $5.75 was
less than the local warehouse price for the material contained in the drum.

The Giant, trying every trick in the book regardless of the morality and legality, failed to
put Evans out of business because of two reasons:

    1.) Evans' versatility and tenacity.
    2.) Foreign steel.

You, our customer, gets better service, better quality and better prices because of foreign
steel. Meanwhile, the arrogant immoral Giant has also become the snivelling Giant that
can't compete with foreign steel price wise, can't compete with foreign steel service wise,
and can't compete with foreign steel quality wise.

Instead of putting its own house in order, it has the audacity to demand that you and the
final consumer hurt yourselves by denying us the use of high quality economically produced
foreign steel. Don't be deceived by The Giant's appeal to patriotism and American job
protection. You need Evans and Evans needs foreign steel.

You will soon receive:
        WHY EVANS COOPERAGE USES FOREIGN STEEL
        EPISODE #3 - TITLE: THE GIANT'S BIG CLUB - RECIPROCITY
                                or
                IF RECIPROCITY DOESN'T KILL EVANS, THE PERVERSION OF IT WIL

EVANS COOPERAGE CO., INC.

POST OFFICE DRAWER 68

MANUFACTURERS AND RECONDITIONERS
OF STEEL SHIPPING CONTAINERS

HARVEY, LOUISIANA 70059

INLAND WATER TERMINAL
AND DRUMMING PLANT

TELEPHONE: 366-8571

October 28, 1977

Enclosed is Episode #3 of Why Evans Cooperage Uses Foreign Steel.

Fortunately for us, the clout of reciprocity has been greatly reduced in recent years; however, The Giant keeps trying.

We were told of an incident of approximately one year ago in which the former president of The Giant's drum manufacturing division attempted to intimidate the purchasing agent of one of the large companies that started to purchase drums from Evans. He was unsuccessful due to the courage of the purchasing agent, who had the support of his superior.

Very truly yours,

EVANS COOPERAGE CO., INC.

Robert G. Evans, President

RGE/bs

Attachment

EVANS COOPERAGE CO., INC.

POST OFFICE DRAWER 68

MANUFACTURERS AND RECONDITIONERS
OF STEEL SHIPPING CONTAINERS

HARVEY, LOUISIANA 70059

INLAND WATER TERMINAL
AND DRUMMING PLANT

TELEPHONE: 366-8571

October 28, 1977

WHY EVANS COOPERAGE USES FOREIGN STEEL

EPISODE #3

TITLE

THE GIANT'S BIG CLUB - RECIPROCITY

or

IF RECIPROCITY DOESN'T KILL EVANS, THE PERVERSION OF IT WILL

Reciprocity will in some fashion always play some part in the buying and selling relationship between certain businesses despite laws to the contrary. Evans is not nor ever has been critical of reciprocal relationships that do not exceed the bounds of fair play and propriety

It is understandable why in the past that if The Giant favored a company by purchasing its products that this same company should favor The Giant with some of its business provided of course that price and service was competitive.

If this is so, why is the practice of reciprocity generally illegal?

Logically, it would appear that it is because of:

1.) The abuse of reciprocity
2.) The perversion of reciprocity

To explain the abuse of reciprocity, consider The Giant and other steel producers who to-gether with their own plants and subsidiary plants were purchasing such enormous amounts of fuel, lubricants and chemicals that they could in many areas demand the lion's share of all the drum business for their own drum manufacturing plants. Service and price were often a secondary factor when a supplier of steel drums was being considered. In areas where the largest percentage of the total business available is dispensed on the basis of reciprocity, the chances of a newcomer lacking reciprocal clout is indeed dismal.

The Giant was not only playing the reciprocity game to the limit abusing it outrageously, but in its effort to eliminate Evans, it decided that the abuse of reciprocity was not decisive enough. The Giant was impatient and as a result decided to pervert the rules of reciprocity.

The New Orleans marketing area was of a type that lent itself very well to the perversion of reciprocity.

First, it has a large market where the abuse of reciprocity could deny Evans a most sub-stantial amount of business.

-1-

continued

October 28, 1977

Secondly, it had a fairly substantial market limited to a very few accounts being principally fillers of vegetable oil and certain petroleum products that were being exported in drums that could not be controlled through reciprocity. Because of the abuse of reciprocity, this market was the only market that Evans could effectively compete in.

The Giant apparently decided that it would hold to full list prices in the reciprocity accounts and drastically cut prices in the few non-reciprocity accounts that were left to Evans.

This perversion of reciprocity not only denied Evans business in the full price reciprocity accounts, BUT ADDITIONALLY FORCED THE RECIPROCITY ACCOUNTS TO FINANCE THE GIANT'S RUTHLESS PRICE CUTTING VENDETTA AGAINST EVANS IN THE NON-RECIPROCITY ACCOUNTS.

If you think the above is unfair, wait until you read:

        WHY EVANS COOPERAGE USES FOREIGN STEEL
        EPISODE #4 - TITLE: THE GIANT ENGAGES IN CHARACTER ASSASSINATION
                                        or
                    THE SAGA OF THE FATHER OF THE THIEF

EVANS COOPERAGE CO., INC.

POST OFFICE DRAWER 68

MANUFACTURERS AND RECONDITIONERS
OF STEEL SHIPPING CONTAINERS

HARVEY, LOUISIANA 70059

INLAND WATER TERMINAL
AND DRUMMING PLANT

TELEPHONE: 366-8571
November 1, 1977

Enclosed is Episode #4 of Why Evans Cooperage Uses Foreign Steel.

The Giant has done much in its efforts to discredit and eliminate Evans; however, it reached a new low in its efforts to malign Evans by engaging in the form of character assassination outlined in the attached Episode #4.

Very truly yours,

EVANS COOPERAGE CO., INC.

Robert G. Evans, President

RGE/bs

Attachment

EVANS COOPERAGE CO., INC.

POST OFFICE DRAWER 68

MANUFACTURERS AND RECONDITIONERS
OF STEEL SHIPPING CONTAINERS

HARVEY, LOUISIANA 70059

INLAND WATER TERMINAL
AND DRUMMING PLANT

November 1, 1977

TELEPHONE: 366-8571

WHY EVANS COOPERAGE USES FOREIGN STEEL

EPISODE #4

TITLE

THE GIANT ENGAGES IN CHARACTER ASSASSINATION

or

THE SAGA OF THE FATHER OF THE THIEF

In 1953 a principal of a large drum reconditioner later to become a drum manufacturer became a stockholder of Evans. Although in very recent years this stock was repurchased by Evans, its principal remained a good friend of the writer until his death.

A number of years ago, while this principal was still a stockholder of Evans, the writer heard of rumors being spread to the effect that Evans was, through this principal, gangster associated.

Cautious inquiries regarding this monstrous lie finally uncovered a source of this rumor. A purchasing agent of one of the major companies whom Evans had helped by furnishing drums during a time when The Giant was on strike, confidentially advised the writer the name of an official of The Giant who visited his office in an effort to oust Evans and did during that visit state that Evans was gangster dominated.

The writer was by that statement placed on the horns of the dilemma in that to punish The Giant and its official for its diabolical statement, the writer would have to violate a promise of confidentiality imposed upon him by the purchasing agent who was in a position to testify.

The enormity of this character assassination was compounded by the fact that the son of this lying Giant official was previously the subject of a lengthy newspaper article naming him as an alleged thief.

The father of the alleged thief, instead of being repentant, was attempting to steal the honor of people who were infinitely more honorable than he or the Giant.

My self respect did not permit me to violate the confidentiality of this purchasing agent, and because of this, The Giant and its dishonorable stooge goes unpunished.

There is a place in hell for individuals like the Giant's lying official, but who ever heard of a corporation going to hell.

-1-

continued

November 1, 1977

If our customers and our government does not keep us from using foreign steel, we may be
able to give The Giant a little hell on earth.

You will soon receive:
            WHY EVANS COOPERAGE USES FOREIGN STEEL
            EPISODE #5 - TITLE: THE HYPOCRITICAL GIANT
                            or
                    LETS SHED CROCODILE TEARS ABOUT PATRIOTISM AND JOB SECURITY

Evans Cooperage Co., Inc.

Post Office Drawer 68

MANUFACTURERS AND RECONDITIONERS
OF STEEL SHIPPING CONTAINERS

Harvey, Louisiana 70059

INLAND WATER TERMINAL
AND DRUMMING PLANT

Telephone: 366-8571
November 4, 1977

Attached is Episode #5 of Why Evans Cooperage Uses Foreign Steel.

While on the subject of hypocrisy, an incident occurring only last week is worth repeating. Last week we purchased 1,000 tons of steel at a very competitive price from a trading firm with whom we had not previously purchased from.

A representative of the firm stated that the steel was manufactured in Spain by a mill that was partially owned by The Giant. If this is so, it is just another example of The Giant's hypocrisy.

If The Giant has funds available for investing in steel mills, it would seem that to be consistent these funds should be invested in its American mills that certainly could use modernization and better management.

Incidentally, The Giant along with other American steel mills have charged the Japanese and most European mills with dumping steel in this country.

We haven't heard of any dumping charges being made against Spanish steel mills. Could it be possible that The Giant is involved in dumping Spanish steel in this country?

If this is so, it would be just another example of The Giant's hypocrisy.

Very truly yours,

EVANS COOPERAGE CO., INC.

Robert G. Evans, President

RGE/bs

Attachment

EVANS COOPERAGE CO., INC.

POST OFFICE DRAWER 68

MANUFACTURERS AND RECONDITIONERS
OF STEEL SHIPPING CONTAINERS

HARVEY, LOUISIANA 70059

INLAND WATER TERMINAL
AND DRUMMING PLANT

November 4, 1977

TELEPHONE: 366-8571

WHY EVANS COOPERAGE USES FOREIGN STEEL

EPISODE #5

TITLE

THE HYPOCRITICAL GIANT

or

LETS SHED CROCODILE TEARS ABOUT PATRIOTISM AND JOB SECURITY

Some years ago a sales official of The Giant visited my office to lecture me regarding my purchasing foreign steel. He stated that in so doing, I was depriving my fellow Americans of jobs in the steel industry.

My two part answer caused him to leave with his tail between his legs. I stated:

 1.) Foreign steel helps me to keep my business alive and provide work for my people.
 2.) How can The Giant criticize Evans for going foreign since in the last few years they had reduced production and employment in some of their American ore mills by purchasing foreign iron ore?

We have recently heard of a confidential rumor from a source that we respect that relates to a visit by the new president of the drum producing subsidiary of The Giant, during which time the new president stated that he was going to request of higher authority permission to purchase foreign steel so that he could become more competitive price wise.

While the hyprocritical Giant equates the purchase of American steel with patriotism and motherhood when addressing the press and governmental regulatory bodies, one of its officials apparently wants to purchase foreign steel to assist it in capturing Evans business.

The Giant has been guilty of much in its effort to break Evans, but who would have ever thought that to accomplish this that they would have considered committing the cardinal sin of purchasing foreign steel.

The Giant does purchase foreign steel and this is how we know.

A few months ago a steel warehouse located in Houston, Texas called our purchasing agent asking if we would be interested in purchasing some steel located at The Giant's New Orleans plant.

Our purchasing agent visited The Giant's plant to inspect the steel, part of which had been rejected. The steel in question was labeled indicating that it was British steel.

Upon questioning the warehouse, it developed that The Giant had purchased 200 tons for one

-1-
continued

November 4, 1977

of its other plants and then purchased an additional 200 tons for its New Orleans plant.
When The Giant feels that purchasing foreign steel suits its purpose, patriotism and job
security goes out the window.

You will soon receive:
                WHY EVANS COOPERAGE USES FOREIGN STEEL
                EPISODE #6 - TITLE: THE GIANT CHANGES HORSES
                                        or
                                BUT IT'S A TROJAN HORSE

EVANS COOPERAGE CO., INC.

POST OFFICE DRAWER 68

MANUFACTURERS AND RECONDITIONERS
OF STEEL SHIPPING CONTAINERS

HARVEY, LOUISIANA 70059

INLAND WATER TERMINAL
AND DRUMMING PLANT

TELEPHONE: 366-8571

November 8, 1977

Attached is Episode #6 on Why Evans Cooperage Uses Foreign Steel.

Forked tongue, who is the subject of this letter, was a most accomplished liar who could look you straight in the eye while lying to you and when he was exposed, never blink an eye while he attempted to cover up by engaging in more lying.

I recall telling this story to a number of people and receiving a reply from one that indicated that he was not surprised since he understood that previously forked tongue had been in deep trouble with the government relating to an alleged illegal act.

Very truly yours,

EVANS COOPERAGE CO., INC.

Robert G. Evans, President

RGE/bs

Attachment

EVANS COOPERAGE CO., INC.

POST OFFICE DRAWER 68

MANUFACTURERS AND RECONDITIONERS
OF STEEL SHIPPING CONTAINERS

HARVEY, LOUISIANA 70059

INLAND WATER TERMINAL
AND DRUMMING PLANT

November 8, 1977

TELEPHONE: 366-8571

WHY EVANS COOPERAGE USES FOREIGN STEEL

EPISODE #6

TITLE

THE GIANT CHANGES HORSES

or

BUT IT'S A TROJAN HORSE

Approximately 4 years ago the writer attended a convention after being informed that The Giant had relieved the president of its drum manufacturing subsidiary of his job.

NOTE: Jones & Laughlin Steel Corporation - Container Division had previously closed its New Orleans plant due to ever mounting losses. Additionally, its president and the president of another drum manufacturing subsidiary of a large steel mill had been relieved of their jobs. The rumor, which seemed reasonable, was that these three presidents had been replaced due to losses sustained by their plants. Meeting the Giant's new president of its drum manufacturing subsidiary, by way of information the writer reviewed his past experiences relating to efforts of The Giant to put Evans out of business.

The writer advised that Evans would continue to resist efforts on the part of The Giant to maintain a two tier price structure - one for reciprocal accounts and a lower price for non-reciprocal accounts.

The new president expressed surprise and sympathy whereupon the writer stated, "when is your company going to stop trying to put us out of business?" The new president, who we will refer to as "forked tongue" (for reasons presented later), stated that whereas he could not discuss prices in a conventional fashion that he would definitely stop the perversion of reciprocity whereby The Giant sold on a two tier system, one for the so called reciprocity accounts and one for the so called non-reciprocity accounts.

Realizing that "forked tongue" was a Giant official, the writer was somewhat skeptical but felt that possibly this official was honest and would keep his promise to stop engaging in the perversion of reciprocity.

Business had been bad for so many years that the writer had decided to invest in a new reconditioning plant and put more emphasis on reconditioning drums. This strategy contemplated some reduction in the number of new drums being produced pending the possibility of government action against The Giant should some independent drum manufacturers fail as a result of The Giant's illegal activities.

It was felt that if Evans could ride out the storm by reliance on its reconditioning plant,

-1-

continued

November 8, 1977

it could later evolve as a strong manufacturer of drums.

In 1973 an unexpected turn of events resulting from a business boom and a worldwide shortage of steel caused a shortage of drums, and because of this, drum prices did increase to list price, the first time since The Giant had cut Evans' prices 15 years before.

During the latter part of 1974 and continuing through 1975, the demand for drums declined drastically. Evans suffered its lowest rate of production in over a decade. Despite this, Evans sold all of its drums at list prices fearing that any deviation of prices on Evans' part would incur the wrath of The Giant and encourage "forked tongue" to resume the perversion of reciprocity.

During that period Evans lost an abnormal amount of business in the non-reciprocity vegetable-petroleum oil business. At first Evans believed that price ceilings that had been invoked prevented "forked tongue" from eliminating the price advantage given these accounts. When price ceilings were removed, it was discovered that "forked tongue" had not only reneged on his promise not to engage in the perversion of reciprocity, but that he had actually attempted to expand it. When questioned by Evans, "forked tongue" attempted to cover his tracks by engaging in bare faced lying.

After many years of marginal profits in manufacturing drums, Evans was now faced with the realization that it could not look forward to anything other than predatory pricing from The Giant. "Forked tongue" is now out and a new president has taken his place. This new president apparently wants to purchase foreign steel to cut Evans' prices, while at the same time complaining about Evans' use of foreign steel.

Fortunately for Evans, the adverse effect of reciprocity has for years been diminishing so that Evans is in a much better position to protect itself against the predatory tactics of The Giant.

Many of our customers, particularly those large producers of fuel, lubricants and chemcials who want to supply the Giant, have responded very well to the service and dependability afforded by Evans and have resisted the efforts of The Giant to secure an unfair advantage.

We have a particular warm place in our heart for one of the larger petroleum companies, who we favored during the steel strike in 1959 by furnishing them drums that they could not get from The Giant whose drum manufacturing plants were on strike.

You will soon receive:
      WHY EVANS COOPERAGE USES FOREIGN STEEL
      EPISODE #7 - TITLE: THE ARROGANT GIANT BECOMES THE UNGRATEFUL GIANT
                              or
          IT BITES THE HAND THAT FEEDS IT

EVANS COOPERAGE CO., INC.

POST OFFICE DRAWER 68

MANUFACTURERS AND RECONDITIONERS
OF STEEL SHIPPING CONTAINERS

HARVEY, LOUISIANA 70059

INLAND WATER TERMINAL
AND DRUMMING PLANT

TELEPHONE: 366-8571

November 11, 1977

The lack of gratitude, which Episode #7 attached indicates, is not confined solely to a customer such as Evans who happens to also be a competitor, but it extends to loyal customers of the Giant that are not competitors.

Not all of the Giant's customers are treated the same regardless of whether they purchase its steel or purchase its drums.

The Giant is seldom grateful. Instead, it can be selective, arbitrary and discriminatory. Many of its suffering customers are beginning to realize it and to object to it.

Very truly yours,

EVANS COOPERAGE CO., INC.

Robert G. Evans, President

RGE/bs

Attachment

EVANS COOPERAGE CO., INC.

POST OFFICE DRAWER 68

MANUFACTURERS AND RECONDITIONERS
OF STEEL SHIPPING CONTAINERS

HARVEY, LOUISIANA 70059

INLAND WATER TERMINAL
AND DRUMMING PLANT

November 11, 1977

TELEPHONE: 366-8571

WHY EVANS COOPERAGE USES FOREIGN STEEL

EPISODE #7

TITLE

THE ARROGANT GIANT BECOMES THE UNGRATEFUL GIANT

or

IT BITES THE HAND THAT FEEDS IT

At one time Evans purchased a substantial part of its steel from the Giant. Instead of being appreciative, the Giant was ungrateful and greedy.

It apparently decided that the revenue from the steel Evans purchased was not enough and that it could increase its revenue by diverting Evans' drum manufacturing business to its own drum manufacturing subsidiary.

Previous episodes of "Why Evans Uses Foreign Steel" have documented some of the Giant's efforts in this regard. The Giant wanted the "Whole Hog" and in engaging in "Biting the Hand that Feeds It", the Giant was acting true to form.

We will illustrate another example of this by reciting below a conversation between the writer and a manager of one of the Giant's drum manufacturing plants.

-In a conversation with this manager soon after a steel price increase, the writer commented upon the practice of the American steel industry to announce a settlement of a contract with the Steel Workers Union and an increase in the price of steel and drums in their drum manufacturing plants over a week end effective the following Monday.

The writer further commented that even though the steel mill would thru their own negligence fail to deliver on schedule as promised and instead deliver after the steel increase was announced that it would insist on billing at the increased price.

At this moment this manager commented by citing a recent incident as an example of the Giant's habit of "Biting the Hand that Feeds it". The incident involved the Giant's manager calling on Friday one of his customers, who had been promised delivery on that Friday, requesting authority to deliver instead on the following Monday. This would enable the Giant to save the cost of working overtime that Friday.

The customer agreed, however, during the weekend steel and drum price increases were announced. The Giant's plant manager appealed to higher authority to bill the drums delivered on Monday at Friday's prices. This plea was denied and the Giant's drum plant manager was forced to penalize a loyal and cooperative customer BY CHARGING HIM THE INCREASED PRICE.

-1-

continued

November 11, 1977

While this loyal customer was being abused by this price increase, other customers of the Giant who were competing with Evans and who were not inhibited by reciprocity did not pay the price increase.

Many of our customers will, we believe, agree that Evans is not the only one that has been abused by the Giant.

You will soon receive:
        WHY EVANS COOPERAGE USES FOREIGN STEEL
        EPISODE #8 - TITLE: THE GIANT FOWLS UP
                        or
        HOW TO SUCCEED THRU INTIMIDATION

Evans Cooperage Co., Inc.

Post Office Drawer 68

MANUFACTURERS AND RECONDITIONERS
OF STEEL SHIPPING CONTAINERS

Harvey, Louisiana 70059

INLAND WATER TERMINAL
AND DRUMMING PLANT

Telephone: 366-8571

November 15, 1977

There is an old saying among customer oriented business people to the effect that the customer is always right. While it is true that this represents some exaggeration, it does reflect a philosophy that is inherently sound and will in the free market place be observed in principal by successful and conscientious business organizations.

The American steel industry has not been exposed long enough to the discipline of the market place to have corrected the bad habits acquired during years of virtual monopoly.

The attached Episode #8 of Why Evans Cooperage Uses Foreign Steel illustrates this.

Very truly yours,

EVANS COOPERAGE CO., INC.

Robert G. Evans, President

RGE/bs

Attachment

Evans Cooperage Co., Inc.

Post Office Drawer 68

MANUFACTURERS AND RECONDITIONERS
OF STEEL SHIPPING CONTAINERS

Harvey, Louisiana 70059

INLAND WATER TERMINAL
AND DRUMMING PLANT

November 15, 1977

Telephone: 366-8571

WHY EVANS COOPERAGE USES FOREIGN STEEL

EPISODE #8

TITLE

THE GIANT FOWLS UP

or

HOW TO SUCCEED THRU INTIMIDATION

It is inevitable and understandable that every steel mill will sooner or later ship some defective steel. Over the years we have purchased steel from the U.S.A., Japan, Korea, Germany, South Africa and France.

Without exception, steel purchased from these foreign countries is of higher quality and contains much less defects than steel which we have purchased from American mills, such as National Steel, Bethlehem Steel, Republic Steel, U.S. Steel and Inland Steel.

When a defect occurs in steel purchased from a foreign source, the representative of the foreign mill is apologetic and eager to settle the claim on an equitable basis. Instead of being remorseful over his admitted inability to equal the quality of foreign producers and settle on an equitable basis, the American mill representative usually enters your plant as an adversary and begins by denying all responsibility except for the most flagrantly defective steel.

The Giant is not alone in this regard; however, we will use as example a typical visit by a Giant adjuster.

By way of explanation, Evans purchases its sheet steel in coils weighing approximately 10,000 pounds. Usually defects in the steel are not apparent as it is received, but instead only becomes apparent as the steel is uncoiled while being processed.(At times the defect may not be noticed even then).

A substantial part of a coil containing defective steel may as it is being uncoiled, give no indication of a defect; however, part way thru, defects may appear. At this point the supervisor realizing that he will lose production if the coil is removed, gambles that the defect may represent only a very small part of the entire coil. If this is true, his production loss will be less than if he had removed the coil.

If, however, a substantial part proves to be defective, he has made two mistakes:

1.) He has lost much more production than if he had removed the coil.

2.) He has given the steel mill adjuster an excuse for denying part of the claim.

November 15, 1977

Referring to condition 2 above, the Giant's adjuster will say, "We will give credit only for that portion of the coil rejected but no credit for your loss time in processing the coil".

Our response is that had we rejected the whole coil, the following would occur:

    1.) The Giant would lose more in the rejected coil than by paying our claim.

    2.) The Giant would not have paid us for the lost production caused by removal of the coil.

The Giant's adjuster after much cross examination agrees to the above statements, but still denies responsibility using a bureaucratic reference to American steel mills adjustment procedures.

I recall during one of the sessions referring to the much higher quality of foreign steel only to have the Giant's adjuster comment. "I realize that the foreigners ship higher qualit steel and we would too, if we were shipping to a distant foreign country and had the exposure of additional expense of a foreign claim".

We have no doubt that the Giant knowingly cuts corners on quality, taking refuge in the following:

    1.) Most, if not all of its American competition, does the same.

    2.) Reciprocity.

    3.) The belief that it can sell a substantial amount of steel despite poor service, low quality and high prices due to the constant threat to the American consumer that a curtailment by our government on the amount of steel imported is inevitable.

The Giant has been wrong about many things, but it is probably right about steel importation being curtailed.

When this occurs, the snivelling Giant will resume its role as the arrogant Giant and the American consumer will pay and pay and pay.

You will soon receive:
    WHY EVANS COOPERAGE USES FOREIGN STEEL
    EPISODE #9 - TITLE: HOW FAR CAN YOU TRUST THE AMERICAN·STEEL INDUSTRY
                             or
          HOW FAR CAN YOU THROW AN ELEPHANT

EVANS COOPERAGE CO., INC.

POST OFFICE DRAWER 68

MANUFACTURERS AND RECONDITIONERS
OF STEEL SHIPPING CONTAINERS

HARVEY, LOUISIANA 70059

INLAND WATER TERMINAL
AND DRUMMING PLANT

November 18, 1977

TELEPHONE: 366-8571

WHY EVANS COOPERAGE USES FOREIGN STEEL

EPISODE #9

TITLE

HOW FAR CAN YOU TRUST THE AMERICAN STEEL INDUSTRY

or

HOW FAR CAN YOU THROW AN ELEPHANT

American industry as a whole has received in recent years considerable criticism regarding its failure to serve the needs of its customers and additionally in failing to follow a path of good ethics and propriety.

Generally speaking, we believe that this criticism is unwarranted. Our experience, however, convinces us that most of the American steel industry is an exception and does lack consideration and morality in its dealing with small consumers of its product.

Over a period of approximately 23 years, we have purchased steel from the following American steel companies: Bethlehem Steel, Republic Steel, Granite City Steel, U.S. Steel, Inland Steel and National Steel.

With one exception, all of these steel companies have failed to deliver as promised at one time or other during a period of shortage. The one exception is National Steel who has been supplying us for less than 3 years and has not been tested during a time of shortage.

Over the years the American steel industry has experienced numerous shortages that usually relate to a strike. The shortage of 1973-74 was an exception to that rule.

Regardless of the reason for the shortage, the pattern of the American steel industry's failure to deliver is basically the same.

A small company such as Evans has been ordering a portion of its requirements from an American mill on a regular basis and does maintain orders on the mill's books months in advance.

Prior to the shortage, the American mill may be operating at 80% of capacity with Evans' orders placed while the mill operates at 80% of capacity. When the shortage develops, the American mill does not cancel Evans' orders, but instead begins to fall back on its delivery schedule.

The plan in instances such as this apparently is to divert a portion of Evans' steel during the shortage to a favored account and to deliver to Evans that portion after the shortage is over.

-1-

continued

EVANS COOPERAGE CO., INC.

POST OFFICE DRAWER 68

MANUFACTURERS AND RECONDITIONERS
OF STEEL SHIPPING CONTAINERS

HARVEY, LOUISIANA 70059

INLAND WATER TERMINAL
AND DRUMMING PLANT

TELEPHONE: 366-8571

November 18, 1977

The monopoly that the American steel industry has enjoyed for so long has hurt it, the consumer, and more particularly the small user of steel.

It can be heart rendering for a small consumer of steel, who has been a loyal customer of an American mill to suffer as a result of that mill to deliver on schedule.

Quite a few years ago American mills did publish on a regular and current basis their production figures.

Knowledge of the figures has enabled Evans in the past to refute a false claim of production delays given by a mill representative to excuse the mills failure to deliver on schedule.

Suddenly the publication of these figures stopped and we have no doubt that the reason was to make it more difficult for a dissatisfied customer to refute such false claims.

Episode #9 of Why Evans Cooperage Uses Foreign Steel, which is attached, does elaborate on the lack of dependability on the part of American mills.

Very truly yours,

EVANS COOPERAGE CO., INC.

Robert G. Evans, President

RGE/bs

Attachment

November 18, 1977

The question that comes to mind is: Why are some accounts favored? In the case of Evans, it cannot be that the mill is incensed over the fact that Evans purchases foreign steel. These incidents of duplicity were just as prevalent in the 8 years prior to Evans purchasing foreign steel as in the years subsequent to such purchases.

We do not know the precise reasons; hence, we must speculate. Our belief is:

    1.) Evans does not purchase enough steel to inhibit the actions of officials who are not conscious enough of their obligations to the consumer.

    2.) Money under the table.

Despite our contempt for the performance of the American steel industry, we do not believe that in most cases the sins of the industry are sins of commission as suggested in #2 above. Instead we are inclined to consider the sins of omission suggested in #1 as the reason for most of the delivery failures to Evans.

An Evans request for the reason for this delay can vary from a claim of a blast furnace break-down to a priority requirement of the U.S. government. A statement by Evans to the effect that Evans placed its order when the mill was operating at 80%, giving the mill a margin of 20% that is certainly more than enough to provide for such contingencies even if they exist, is not very embarassing to many of these representatives who pretend to be oblivious of the mill's duplicity.

It is, however, to the credit of some of these representatives that they are embarassed enough and ashamed enough to apologize off the record.

This realization and admission of mill duplicity cannot be used against the mill because of the confidential nature of the disclosure. It is doubtful that if it was used against them, it would be of any real help. Allocations of steel during a period of shortage are often made by officials who have a thick skin and a thin conscious.

In Episode #10, which you will soon receive, we will document some of the more flagrant examples of the failure of American mills to deliver as promised during a period of shortage.

    WHY EVANS COOPERAGE USES FOREIGN STEEL
    EPISODE #10 - TITLE: THE GREAT AMERICAN STEEL INDUSTRY SHELL GAME
                       or
            SOMEONE ELSE GETS YOUR STEEL WHEN THE MARKET IS TIGHT

EVANS COOPERAGE CO., INC.

POST OFFICE DRAWER 68

MANUFACTURERS AND RECONDITIONERS
OF STEEL SHIPPING CONTAINERS

HARVEY, LOUISIANA 70059

INLAND WATER TERMINAL
AND DRUMMING PLANT

TELEPHONE: 366-8571

November 22, 1977

Attached is Episode #10 on Why Evans Cooperage Uses Foreign Steel.

We are confident that large purchasers of steel, such as the automotive and appliance industry are not amongst the victims of the Great American Steel Industry Shell Game. They have enough market clout to inhibit the performance of these shell game artists.

The victims are small consumers of steel such as Evans, who are expendable and therefore fair game. It is incredible and we know hard to believe that in 23 years of purchasing steel from American steel mills that produce the great majority of American steel that Evans has not found one producer that has consistently kept its promise to deliver during a time of shortage.

Sometimes Evans feels like that old Greek with the lantern.

Very truly yours,

EVANS COOPERAGE CO., INC.

(Robert G. Evans, President

RGE/bs

Attachment

Evans Cooperage Co., Inc.

POST OFFICE DRAWER 68

MANUFACTURERS AND RECONDITIONERS
OF STEEL SHIPPING CONTAINERS

HARVEY, LOUISIANA 70059

INLAND WATER TERMINAL
AND DRUMMING PLANT

TELEPHONE: 366-8571

November 22, 1977

WHY EVANS COOPERAGE USES FOREIGN STEEL

EPISODE #10

TITLE

THE GREAT AMERICAN STEEL INDUSTRY SHELL GAME

or

SOMEONE ELSE GETS YOUR STEEL WHEN THE MARKET IS TIGHT

CASE #1

Episode #1 dated October 21, 1977 relates of Evans' unsuccessful efforts to purchase steel from 4 of the American giant steel producers, who also manufactured steel drums.

Evans finally succeeded in purchasing steel from a midwestern steel producer, who we will refer to as Traitor.

When Evans started to purchase from Traitor, it was only using steel in gauges lighter than 18 gauge, which could only be purchased as cold rolled steel. Later when Evans started producing 18 gauge drums, all of its purchase in 18 gauge or heavier could be made elsewhere in cheaper hot rolled steel that by that time became readily available.

Despite the fact that market conditions made the purchase of cheaper hot rolled steel an economic requirement, Evans did out of gratitude to Traitor continue to purchase from Traitor at a considerable sacrifice a substantial portion of its 18 gauge steel as more expensive cold rolled steel.

Traitor, which could not supply Evans with 18 gauge hot rolled steel, swore undying gratitude to Evans for its sacrifice in paying Traitor a premium.

The first time that a shortage developed, Traitor initiated Evans into the Great American Steel Industry Shell Game - they delayed delivery and invented excuses that Evans wanted to believe.

Later, during the lengthy steel strike of 1959, Traitor did it again. That ended Evans' business relationship with Traitor and now you know why Evans labels that midwest steel mill Traitor.

CASE #2

Evans was purchasing a substantial part of its steel from a steel mill that also owned a drum manufacturing plant in the New Orleans area. A large shipment of steel ordered by Evans from

November 22, 1977

this mill, which we will refer to as Double Crosser, was scheduled for shipment by barge just prior to the start of the lengthy steel strike of 1959.

As the deadline for the strike approached, Evans became apprehensive and contacted Double Crosser, who promised to do its best to load the barge before the strike started. Just after the strike started, Evans again contacted Double Crosser and was advised that the steel WAS READY FOR SHIPMENT BUT HAD NOT BEEN LOADED.

The strike was a lengthy one, with Double Crosser's New Orleans drum plant being also shut down by the strike. Evans, meanwhile, operated throughout the strike utilizing a large stockpile of steel purchased in anticipation.

Just after the strike ended, a representative of Double Crosser's New Orleans drum plant, who Evans knew quite well, called Evans stating that they had miscalculated earlier and had failed to place orders for steel before the strike and was as a result short of steel. This representative wanted to borrow steel from Evans, who replied that he could lend the steel conditioned upon an assurance that it could be replaced promptly.

There are honest people in the steel industry and this party was one of them. He stated that despite his needing the steel badly, he could not borrow it under false pretenses. Due to their error in not ordering steel from their parent Double Crosser prior to the strike, they could not expect more steel for quite a few weeks. This would prevent the early replacement that was Evans' condition in lending the steel.

Evans then contacted Double Crosser about its steel, asking if it was being loaded aboard a barge. Evans received the old double talk routine that the American steel industry has developed to perfection. The shell game was being replayed and it was obvious that Evans' steel was being diverted elsewhere and Evans had a good idea where.

Evans employed a detective agency to check Double Crosser's New Orleans drum manufacturing plant and sure enough the Evans steel arrived on schedule at Double Crosser's plant.

As I recall it, Jesus Christ said something to the effect that a rich man had less chance in going to heaven than a camel had in going through the eye of a needle.

Had there been an American steel industry around when Jesus made that statement, he probably would have had a substitution for the rich man.

You will soon receive:
          WHY EVANS COOPERAGE USES FOREIGN STEEL
          EPISODE #11 - TITLE: EVANS ALSO BUYS AMERICAN STEEL - WHY?
                              or
                    FOR EVANS IT'S A SHOT GUN MARRIAGE

EVANS COOPERAGE CO., INC.

POST OFFICE DRAWER 68

MANUFACTURERS AND RECONDITIONERS
OF STEEL SHIPPING CONTAINERS

INLAND WATER TERMINAL
AND DRUMMING PLANT

HARVEY, LOUISIANA 70059

TELEPHONE: 366-8571

November 25, 1977

Since the first part of 1975 and during a time when steel was very plentiful, Evans has paid in excess of $500,000.00 in premiums to purchase American steel. Part of this money could have been in our pocket and part of it could have been in your company's pocket.

This $500,000.00 plus is in effect insurance which Evans pays to insure itself against sabotage.

Evans believes that the free enterprise system in America, when it relates to the American steel industry, will be sabotaged by a coalition of the American steel industry and labor.

Episode #11, attached, is in explanation.

Very truly yours,

EVANS COOPERAGE CO., INC.

Robert G. Evans, President

RGE/bs

Attachment

Evans Cooperage Co., Inc.

Post Office Drawer 68

MANUFACTURERS AND RECONDITIONERS
OF STEEL SHIPPING CONTAINERS

Harvey, Louisiana 70059

INLAND WATER TERMINAL
AND DRUMMING PLANT

November 25, 1977

Telephone: 366-8571

WHY EVANS COOPERAGE USES FOREIGN STEEL

EPISODE #11

TITLE

EVANS ALSO BUYS AMERICAN STEEL - WHY?

or

FOR EVANS IT'S A SHOT GUN MARRIAGE

In the ten previous episodes there has been documented an incredible array of incidents that literally constitute an inditement of not just one company but virtually the entire American steel industry. Evans has obviously been hurt in the process.

Despite all of this, Evans continues to purchase substantial amounts of American steel. Why is this so? Evans is proud of its unexcelled record of performance, unblemished in over 20 years of drum production. It has never failed to supply its customers regardless of steel shortage or other emergencies.

In recent years it has become very apparent that the American steel industry has aligned itself with labor to form a powerful lobby that may very well re-create at least in part the complete domination that the domestic steel industry formally enjoyed.

In all probability this lobby in the near future is going to substantially reduce the amount of foreign steel available to people like Evans and for the past several years Evans has been paying tribute as a hedge against this possibility. It has been purchasing second rate higher priced steel, purchased as Class I steel at full list price, the majority of which comes from an American steel company, which Evans hopes will prove an exception to the rule in morality if not in quality of its product.

It is costing Evans money now and it is going to cost you in the future. We predict that if the importation of foreign steel is seriously curtailed and if business improved moderately in 1978 that there will be a steel shortage in this country by the end of 1978.

Because of this, Evans has substantially increased its purchase of steel for delivery during the next 7 months. Our projection is an inventory in excess of 13,000 tons of steel by June of 1978 equal to our requirements for approximately 8 months.

This inventory should provide an adequate cushion to enable us to weather the possible shortage referred to above.

-1-

continued

November 25, 1977

The monopoly we fear, like all monopolies, must inevitably fail. Until that day arrives, you, Evans and our country must live with higher prices and lower quality.

You will soon receive:
      WHY EVANS COOPERAGE USES FOREIGN STEEL
      EPISODE #12 - TITLE: THE HYPOCRISY INVOLVED IN DUMPING CHARGES
                              or
            LET HE WHO IS WITHOUT SIN CAST THE FIRST STONE

EVANS COOPERAGE CO., INC.

POST OFFICE DRAWER 68

MANUFACTURERS AND RECONDITIONERS
OF STEEL SHIPPING CONTAINERS

HARVEY, LOUISIANA 70059

INLAND WATER TERMINAL
AND DRUMMING PLANT

TELEPHONE: 366-8571

November 29, 1977

On November 15, 1977 I read one of Art Buchwald's humorous articles involving an American steel mill lobbyist's hypocrisy. Enclosed is a copy of that article.

There is, of course, some exaggeration, but we feel that it is closer to reality than many believe.

Episode #12 attached indicates another facet of the hypocrisy of the American steel industry.

Very truly yours,

EVANS COOPERAGE CO., INC.

Robert G. Evans, President

RGE/bs

Attachments

quality and service expectations.

Please come and see our Columbus and New Orleans operations. We are proud of our facilities and would like to not only show you our plants and meet some of our people, but also when in New Orleans we would like to show you something about our interesting city.

Best regards,

EVANS INDUSTRIES, INC.

Ronald J. Evans, President

p.s. Enclosed please find a book about my father's life. He was one of the real innovators and characters of our industry. I believe you will find the book easy to read and interesting.

Doc:Bernie Stinson – Superior Solvents

P.O. Drawer 68 • 1255 Peters Road • Harvey, LA 70059
Phone: (504) 374-6000 • Fax: (504) 374-6001

ISO9002
REGISTERED COMPANY

NATIONAL
ACCREDIATION
OF CERTIFICATION
BODIES

June 30, 1999

Mr. Bernie Stinson
Superior Solvents and Chemicals
4211 Bramers Lane
Louisville, Kentucky 40216

Dear Bernie:

Jim Phillips and I really appreciate the time that you gave us during our recent trip to Superior's Louisville facility.

You have reason to be proud of your plant and the improvements that you have been making. The operation is very flexible and does some very interesting things, more than most standard chemical distribution facilities do that I have seen in the past. Keep up the good work!

We had a good visit with Michelle Wilson in Cincinnati and Jay Baker in Indianapolis. We hope to be able to supply Superior with both high quality reconditioned and new drums in the future. We really appreciate your candid comments about what we need to do to improve our service. I am confident that if we have another opportunity to supply your facility that we will meet your

EVANS COOPERAGE CO., INC.

POST OFFICE DRAWER 68

MANUFACTURERS AND RECONDITIONERS
OF STEEL SHIPPING CONTAINERS

HARVEY, LOUISIANA 70059

INLAND WATER TERMINAL
AND DRUMMING PLANT

November 29, 1977

TELEPHONE: 366-8571

WHY EVANS COOPERAGE USES FOREIGN STEEL

EPISODE #12

TITLE

THE HYPOCRISY INVOLVED IN DUMPING CHARGES

or

LET HE WHO IS WITHOUT SIN CAST THE FIRST STONE

The American steel industry has already been partially successful and will probably be increasingly successful in reducing competition by the use of anti-dumping legislation.

These hypocrites say that it is unfair for the foreign mills to sell in America at less than their cost plus a reasonable profit. At the same time they are in effect dumping steel on the American market and here is how they do it.

Evans purchases 600 tons of steel per month from an American mill. This steel, which is inferior in quality to foreign steel is purchased at full list price and no consideration is given to Evans price wise for its loyalty in consistently and continually purchasing that 600 tons each and every month.

Evans can, however, purchase that same steel at a considerable discount through a steel broker or warehouse. At the profit level of this mill, it is obvious that the steel is sold at less than cost plus a reasonable profit. When confronted, the average American mill representative resorts to double talk and subterfuge that would put a second class used car salesman to shame.

Amongst other things, he will say something like, "we are selling this warehouse secondary rejected steel which our policy does not permit us to sell to a consumer".

The duplicity involved in this statement is apparent when this broker or warehouse guarantees that "YOU CAN ORDER FROM HIM THE EXACT SIZE, QUANTITY AND SPECIFICATION YOU REQUIRE".

When the foreigner dumps, the customer gets the entire benefit of the reduced price from an appreciative supplier. When an American dumps, it is through a favorite broker or warehouse who peddles it at times like it is a hot late model automobile.

We won't comment on why a broker operating out of his hip pocket can purchase American steel originating at an American mill at less than a loyal customer. We are confident the reasons vary from mill to mill and from time to time. Suggest you come to your own conclusion.

-1-

continued

November 29, 1977

No matter how thin you slice it, it's dumping just the same.

You will soon receive:
        WHY EVANS COOPERAGE USES FOREIGN STEEL
         EPISODE #13 - TITLE: WHY THE U.S. STEEL INDUSTRY CAN'T COMPETE
                            or
                 A MONOPOLY WILL SAP YOUR STRENGTH AND YOUR MORAL FIBRE

EVANS COOPERAGE CO., INC.

POST OFFICE DRAWER 68

MANUFACTURERS AND RECONDITIONERS
OF STEEL SHIPPING CONTAINERS

HARVEY, LOUISIANA 70059

INLAND WATER TERMINAL
AND DRUMMING PLANT

TELEPHONE: 366-8571
December 2, 1977

If you had heard that there was an American industrial corporation that was so huge and
so profitable that its profits were greater than the combined profits of the next six
American industrial corporations, you probably could not and would not believe it. If
in addition you are told that this same corporation, although remaining generally very
profitable, would in two generations be unable to compete with companies abroad, you
probably would not believe that either.

Truth is sometimes stranger than fiction and what we refer to above has actually happened.
We believe that you will find the attached September 15, 1917 copy of the top 100
industrials for 1917 interesting.

Episode #13, which is attached, gives some detail on this and other American steel
companies.

Very truly yours,

EVANS COOPERAGE CO., INC.

Robert G. Evans, President

RGE/bs

Attachments

EVANS COOPERAGE CO., INC.

POST OFFICE DRAWER 68

MANUFACTURERS AND RECONDITIONERS
OF STEEL SHIPPING CONTAINERS

HARVEY, LOUISIANA 70059

TELEPHONE: 366-8571

INLAND WATER TERMINAL
AND DRUMMING PLANT

December 2, 1977

WHY EVANS COOPERAGE USES FOREIGN STEEL

EPISODE #13

TITLE

WHY THE U.S. STEEL INDUSTRY CAN'T COMPETE

or

A MONOPOLY WILL SAP YOUR STRENGTH AND YOUR MORAL FIBRE

The American steel industry not too many years ago the largest, strongest, richest and most efficient steel industry in the world is now unable to compete with foreign mills.

Attached is a list of the performance of the 100 top industrials in America in 1917. Note that U.S. Steel #1 earned in one year 224.2 million dollars. In todays ability to build a modern steel mill this 224.2 million dollars would equal approximately 2 billion dollars. In 1917 U.S. Steel earned an incredible profit that was greater than THE COMBINED PROFITS OF THE NEXT 6 AMERICAN INDUSTRIAL CORPORATIONS. Today U.S. Steel indicates it doesn't have enough money to modernize and blames the foreigners.

Note that Bethlehem Steel and Midvale Steel which later merged, had profits totalling 62.9 million ranking just behind Standard Oil (N.J.) which was then #2. Bethlehem is today losing money in part because of the obsolescence of some of its plants and blaming the foreigners.

Although it was the 8th largest steel company and the 53rd largest industrial company, Youngstown Sheet and Tube earned 38.4 million dollars on 98 million dollars of revenue. THIS WAS A PROFIT OF OVER 40% ON REVENUE. Today Youngstown (Lykes Youngstown) is losing money and closing down a substantial part of its ancient inefficient plant capacity, meanwhile it blames the foreigners.

Note that all 11 of the steel companies listed in the first 100 industrials were extremely profitable and that their combined profits totalled 436.6 million dollars or ALMOST ONE HALF OF THE 1062.5 MILLION DOLLARS EARNED IN TOTAL BY THE 89 OTHER INDUSTRIALS LISTED IN THE FIRST 100.

Where did all the money earned by the American steel industry go and why can't this industry compete today? We believe the reason is that for too long they enjoyed a virtual monopoly. Monopoly, which because we are human, tempts all businessmen singing the serene song of an easier life and higher profits. Monopoly does for a while deliver, but while it is delivering, it is undermining the strength and moral fibre of its proponents.

The American steel industry in effect formed an alliance with labor to create a virtual

continued

December 2, 1977

monopoly that worked for a while to their mutual benefit at the expense of the American consumer and a majority of the American workers.

At one time the various members of the American steel industry did not compete price wise charging every consumer regardless of location the same FOB mill price plus transportation from Pittsburg to consumer location. Meanwhile the greater part of the American steel industry bargained as a unit with the union - agreeing to reduced efficiency and unreasonable wages with the assurance that their position of virtaul monopoly permitted them to pass on this increased cost to the defenseless consumer.

It was all so cosy enabling aging, inefficient plants to survive and profit, permitting steel executives and labor leaders to throw their weight around, and producing an elite work force that worked less and earned more than their less fortunate brothers.

In the early 1960's, an ominous cloud appeared on the horizon in the form of foreign competition that would not conform to the rules of "the consumer be dammed". Foreign mills started to ship higher quality, lower priced steel into this country and to top it all actually began to treat the small American consumer with courtesy and consideration.

To meet this competition, those plutocrats of industry and labor who controlled the American steel industry should have and could have reacted decisively and intelligently. They could have mended their ways and mended their plants.

Had they done so, the American steel industry of today would be the strongest and healthiest in the world and consumers like Evans would be loyal and willing customers.

This sick industry has a sick solution to all of its problems. It wants to severely restrict the importation of foreign steel. If it succeeds in recreating this same monopolistic enviro ment that we believe caused its problems in the first place, it will merely postpone the inevitable.

Enclosed also is a photostat from the November 14, 1977 issue of the Wall Street Journal indicating a desire on the part of U.S. Steel to reduce steel imports to "a trickle".

The result will be a less efficient, more arrogant, weaker industry aligned with a politicall stronger group of labor, who, if they are not inhibited by a return of competition may well eventually promote the nationalization of the American steel industry.

The American steel industry should take heed.

The mills of the Gods grind slowly, but they grind exceedingly fine.

Evans Cooperage Co., Inc.

POST OFFICE DRAWER 68

MANUFACTURERS AND RECONDITIONERS
OF STEEL SHIPPING CONTAINERS

HARVEY, LOUISIANA 70059

INLAND WATER TERMINAL
AND DRUMMING PLANT

TELEPHONE: 368-6000

October 3, 1978

During the latter part of 1977, I forwarded to your company 13 episodes of "Why Evans uses Foreign Steel."

Whereas, most of the emphasis was directed towards the predatory tactics of "The Giant", there were references to the immorality of certain phases of American steel industry activity that seem to be the result of concerted action at high managerial levels.

Please read the attached Episode #14 entitled:

THE GIANT IS NOT ALONE

or

INLAND ALSO ENGAGES IN CHARACTER ASSASSINATION

Episode #14 represents just another illustration of the hostility and worse that Evans has had to cope with in manufacturing and selling drums in competition with the majors. It should be evaluated not as a single incident, but instead as part of a long history of misrepresentation and harassment as contained in the previous 13 episodes. As a matter of fact you will receive Episode #15 soon, reciting another incident with another American steel producer.

Very truly yours,

EVANS COOPERAGE COMPANY, INC.

Robert G. Evans
President

RGE:rb

Evans Cooperage Co., Inc.

Post Office Drawer 68

MANUFACTURERS AND RECONDITIONERS
OF STEEL SHIPPING CONTAINERS

Harvey, Louisiana 70059

INLAND WATER TERMINAL
AND DRUMMING PLANT

Telephone: 368-6000

October 3, 1978

WHY EVANS COOPERAGE USES FOREIGN STEEL

EPISODE # 14

TITLE

THE GIANT IS NOT ALONE

or

INLAND ALSO ENGAGES IN CHARACTER ASSASSINATION

On Thursday, September 28th, a representative of Inland's New Orleans drum manufacturing plant called an Evans' representative asking if Evans would lend them 300, 12 gauge bolt locking rings to be used on open head drums.

Evans agreed, as it has many times in the past, and shortly thereafter Inland's driver arrived to pick up the rings and presented a hand written memo which stated "300 - 12 gauge bolt locking rings, 12" X 46" (a photo of that sheet is enclosed).

Our Plant Manager was surprised and appalled at the type written message contained on the other side of this memo; particularly at the contents of the third sentence of paragraph #2, "WE ARE IN A SURVIVAL WAR WITH EVANS AND FLORIDA DRUM, WHO HAVE CUT PRICES TO TAKE AS MUCH BUSINESS AS THEY CAN FROM US AND FORCE THE PRICES DOWN ON WHAT IS LEFT SO THAT WE CANNOT SURVIVE IN THE CONTAINER BUSINESS."

Evans knows little about Florida Drum's operation and therefore can say little about them, except to state unequivocally, that Evans did not in any shape or form conspire with Florida Drum to put Inland out of business; or to, in any way, plan or discuss with Florida Drum any method to harm Inland or to take any of Inland's business.

This Inland document, which was obviously given wide spread publicity within its plant fails to mention the real culprit which is the Giant, who in its effort to eliminate Evans, may be on the verge of eliminating Inland, if indeed Inland is being truthful regarding its difficulty in surviving in New Orleans.

The duplicity in not naming the Giant is compounded by the fact that Inland officials have in the past, on more than one occassion, stated to me directly and emphatically, that they recognized the Giant as the culprit.

There is probably more than one reason why Jay, the Inland Plant Manager, did not name the Giant as the real culprit, however, we feel that he was influenced by the belief that he would seriously offend his superiors if he did so.

October 3, 1978

This Inland document does more than malign Evans and accuse Evans of illegal activities. It suggests that Inland's New Orleans plant is in trouble and may not survive.

If that part of the statement is true, then Inland customers may be concerned. If it is not true, then Inland has deceived its employees in addition to maligning Evans.

You will soon receive:

WHY EVANS COOPERAGE USES FOREIGN STEEL

EPISODE #15 - TITLE: IF YOU BUY AMERICAN STEEL BE WARY

or

IT HELPS TO HAVE EYES IN THE BACK
OF YOUR HEAD

EVANS COOPERAGE CO., INC.

POST OFFICE DRAWER 68

MANUFACTURERS AND RECONDITIONERS
OF STEEL SHIPPING CONTAINERS

HARVEY, LOUISIANA 70059

INLAND WATER TERMINAL
AND DRUMMING PLANT

TELEPHONE: 368-6000

October 12, 1978

Recently it came to our attention that one of the major steel companies did in the latter part of 1977 announce a policy change that limited its responsibility for shortages that might develop due to mill inaccuracy in measuring steel sold on a theoretical basis.

We do not know why they made the change, however, after reading the attached Episode #15 it is possible that you may wonder if the change was made as a result of their being caught too often with their hands in the cookie jar.

Very truly yours,

EVANS COOPERAGE CO., INC.

Robert G. Evans, President

RGE/bs

Attachment

Evans Cooperage Co., Inc.

Post Office Drawer 68

MANUFACTURERS AND RECONDITIONERS
OF STEEL SHIPPING CONTAINERS

Harvey, Louisiana 70059

INLAND WATER TERMINAL
AND DRUMMING PLANT

Telephone: 368-6000

October 12, 1978

WHY EVANS COOPERAGE USES FOREIGN STEEL

EPISODE #15

TITLE

IF YOU BUY AMERICAN STEEL BE WARY

or

IT HELPS TO HAVE EYES IN THE BACK OF YOUR HEAD

Earlier episodes of why Evans purchases foreign steel recited some of the incidents of duplicity that Evans has experienced in dealing with the American Steel Industry.

Until it started doing business with its present large American supplier of steel in mid 1975, it had been abused in one fashion or another by every American steel producer from whom it had purchased steel.

When in early 1975 Evans proposed a long time relationship with the American mill that is the subject of this episode, Evans recited in detail its previous experiences and expressed a desire and a need for a relationship with an American mill that it could respect and trust.

Evans explained that there were two basic reasons for this desire and need:

    1.) Evans was convinced that pressure from the American Steel Industry and from labor would result in some substantial curtailment of imported steel.

    2.) Evans was a staunch believer of the capitalistic system and did so badly want to believe that there were still some American steel producers who could be trusted.

Needless to say, the representative of this mill indicated a desire to convince Evans that it was an exception and that Evans would be taken care of. In later conversations with this representative, when Evans expressed a concern for the future, Evans was informed by this same representative that Evans need not fear, THAT EVANS WAS DEALING WITH A MILL THAT SPECIALIZED IN STEEL SHEETS AND THAT EVANS PURCHASED A BARGELOAD OF 600 TONS PER MONTH OF A TYPE OF STEEL THAT HAD NON-CRITICAL SPECIFICATIONS, WAS EASY TO PRODUCE, AND VERY PROFIT-ABLE. He concluded with a statement to the effect that this fact was our best protection, regardless of how I felt or what he or his mill promised. I replied that if his mill oper-ated in the same fashion that other American mills whom I had dealt with, that his statement would represent Evans' best protection but that I hoped to develop a relationship with an American mill based on trust rather than cynicism.

October 12, 1978

In 1976 and 1977 business declined substantially and the Giant continued to cut prices in those areas where Evans sold most of its drums. Evans needed the price advantage of foreign steel and never stopped purchasing a substantial part of its requirement from foreign steel producers. Despite these substantial savings amounting to in some instances over 2¢ per pound, Evans continued without ever failing to accept one shipment to purchase 600 or more tons per month from this American mill. This pattern continued thru 1977.

Evans purchases American steel on a theoretical basis, which means that it orders by the pound at a price quoted by the pound, however, it is billed according to a formula that assesses Evans on the basis of area of steel delivered by the mill.

Evans keeps very detailed records of steel received and maintains identity of each coil until it is consumed. By counting the number of sheets from the coil containing body stock and by counting the number of drum heads cut from coils containing head stock, Evans can determine very precisely the accuracy of any billing made on a theoretical basis.

Whereas Evans had been keeping these records for years and had never stopped keeping these detailed records, Evans became complacent and did in mid 75 stop compiling from these records the data available to it.

It had been lulled into a false sense of security by the accuracy and ethics of the Japanese, and it had checked the first one or two shipments made by this American mill and found the yield to be satisfactory.

In late 1977 Evans started to compile the data available to it on all steel received and was appalled to find out that every shipment received after the first two shipments from this American mill was short shipped resulting in Evans being overbilled by this one mill A TOTAL OF $127,290.02.

Evans was outraged, demanded a complete investigation including a visit to our plant to check our records and our procedures. At least two visits were made to our plant by mill representatives who were favorably impressed by our system. After Evans sent to the mill a voluminous set of records, the mill did months later permit Evans to deduct $127,290.02 from a shipment of steel made in August of 1978.

The mill's excuse for the overcharge was that it had no accurate method to measure the linear feet (or area) of steel shipped and that the mill billed on a theoretical basis using a complicated formula based on average yield at the mill.

The mill could not explain an incredible pattern of billing, which resulted in THE FIRST TWO SHIPMENTS HAVING NO SHORTAGES AND THAT ON EVERYONE OF THE BALANCE OF APPROXIMATELY 28 SHIPMENTS SUBSEQUENTLY MADE, EVANS WAS SHORT CHANGED.

Evans is still purchasing steel from that same mill since it seems unlikely that it can find an American mill where it can rely on trust rather than cynicism.

Evans Cooperage Co., Inc.

Post Office Drawer 68

MANUFACTURERS AND RECONDITIONERS
OF STEEL SHIPPING CONTAINERS

Harvey, Louisiana 70059

INLAND WATER TERMINAL
AND DRUMMING PLANT

Telephone: 368-6000

October 18, 1978

For many years the United States was a net exporter of steel. Continued success in an export market, however, does require extra effort and an entrepreneurial approach to selling that does not thrive in a complacent atmosphere.

During the early sixties the effect of years of monopoly such as referred to in Episode #13 had begun to take its toll even though the American Steel Industry was still enjoying prosperity unaffected by foreign competition.

Attached is Episode #16 on why Evans buys foreign steel that provides one illustration of the folly of complacency.

Incredible as it may seem, the Giant ignored common sense, the advice of its international manager, the welfare of its workers and its own future in refusing to seriously compete in an export market that was practically at their back door.

Very truly yours,

EVANS COOPERAGE CO., INC.

Robert G. Evans, President

RGE/bs

Attachment

EVANS COOPERAGE CO., INC.

POST OFFICE DRAWER 68

MANUFACTURERS AND RECONDITIONERS
OF STEEL SHIPPING CONTAINERS

HARVEY, LOUISIANA 70059

INLAND WATER TERMINAL
AND DRUMMING PLANT

TELEPHONE: 368-6000

October 18, 1978

WHY EVANS COOPERAGE USES FOREIGN STEEL

EPISODE #16

TITLE

A GLIMPSE INTO THE REALM OF FOOLS PARADISE

or

WHEN IGNORANCE IS BLISS IT'S FOLLY TO BE WISE

In the late fifties Evans was providing drums and drumming service for a large American Refinery that was shipping asphalt in bulk to Evans, who drummed the material and delivered it shipside at New Orleans for export.

One day an official from a subsidiary of this company called me asking if I would visit their Venezuelan refinery as a consultant. He wanted my advice as to why their Venezuelan refinery, a large modern refinery operating off of cheap asphaltic crude could not compete in the Caribbean with asphalt produced in their parent's Louisiana refinery and shipped through the Evans plant.

My reply was that the basic reason was obvious. By far the greater part of the cost of drummed asphalt was contained in the drums and drumming service. Since this official had access to details as to our costs and their Venezuelan costs, determination could be defined very easily without my visit to their refinery.

This official agreed in principle but felt that the expense of my visit and analysis would be justified by a more detailed on site visit by me.

I agreed and spent two days at the refinery observing and partially preparing my report. The cost of the drums being produced in Venezuela by a large Dutch drum manufacturer, who used steel imported into Venezuela, was considerably more expensive than Evans drums.

To complete my report I did, upon my return, check into the cost of European, Japanese and American steel delivered into Venezuela.

To get the price of American steel delivered to the port of New Orleans, I called the manager of the Giant's International Division reciting the exact reason for my inquiry.

Upon receiving the price I indicated surprise that the price of steel delivered by the Giant to New Orleans for export was higher than the same type of steel delivered to New Orleans for domestic production of drums. When the manager of the Giant's International Division could not justify economically this price differential, I made the following comments:

1.) His company should definitely be competitive in the export market since the

October 18, 1978

additional tonnage so generated would enable it to operate its plants at optimum capacity thereby reducing its costs and additionally providing full employment for its employees.

    2.) Success in #1 above would provide additional funds for modernization and by providing full employment improve its posture in dealing with their union.

    3.) Whereas foreign and more particularly the Japanese were not then competing very strongly in the United States, they were expanding their plants and taking away from the Americans a substantial part of their export market.

    4.) By playing into the hands of these foreign producers in overcharging on its export shipments, the Giant was substantially contributing to the economic strength of these foreigners WHO WOULD IN A VERY FEW YEARS MOVE INTO THE AMERICAN MARKET AND CAPTURE A LARGE PART OF IT.

The reply of this manager of the Giant was, "Mr. Evans, you know this and I know this, but my superiors will not listen to me when I approach them along the lines of your observations. Would you please tell them this for me?"

I did not tell them, since as subtitle to this episode indicates "WHEN IGNORANCE IS BLISS IT'S FOLLY TO BE WISE".